BORN IN 1975

WORD SEARCH

THIS BOOK

BELONGS TO

D'Azur®
Publishing

ELIZABETH ABSALOM & MALCOLM WATSON

D'AZUR PUBLISHING

BORN IN 1975 WORD SEARCH

Published by D'Azur Publishing 2025
D'Azur Publishing is a Division of D'Azur Limited

The language, phrases and terminology within this book are as written at the time of the news reports during the year covered and convey and illustrate the sentiments at that time, even though modern society may find some words inappropriate. The news reports are taken from internationally recognised major newspapers and other sources of the year in question. The language does not represent any personal view of the author or publisher.

First published in Great Britain in 2025 by D'Azur Limited
Contact: info@d-azur.com Visit www.d-azur.com

ISBN 9798307338131

ACKNOWLEDGEMENTS
The publisher wishes to acknowledge the following people and sources:

Layout & puzzles by Amanda Dean

British Newspaper Archive; The Times Archive; p10 (Liberty's Facade) Jon; p10 (Liberty's Sign) James G; p26 (Evacuation) Hubert van Es; p38 Edinburgh Fringe Festival; p50 Vintage Dancer; p56 MacDonalds; p62 Vintage Dancer; p84 Science Museum; p84 Jody Kingzett; p86 NASA; P46 Salvatore Barbera; p94 Eduard Marmet airliners.net; p98 Wadhurst History Society.

Whilst we have made every effort to contact copyright holders, should we have made any omission, please contact us so that we can make the appropriate acknowledgement.

D'Azur Publishing ®

D'Azur Limited

CONTENTS

Every puzzle is based on the stories printed on the facing page.

EASIER puzzles have words that go horizontally forwards and backwards and also upwards and downwards. Letters may be used in more than one word.

HARDER puzzles have words that can go in any direction - horizontally, vertically and diagonally, both forwards and backwards. Letters may be used in more than one word.

LIFE IN 1975 - 1

Monarch: Queen Elizabeth II   Prime Minister: Ted Heath (Conservative) From March 4th Harold Wilson (Labour)

In 1975 the Sex Discrimination and Equal Pay Acts paved the way for a fairer society. Bill Gates founded Microsoft at the age of 19, and Margaret Thatcher became the first woman leader of the Conservative party.

The weather was equally astonishing with snow showers as far south as London in June. The Sex Pistols made their debut in November establishing Punk Rock on the music scene, while on the TV we watched Fawlty Towers.

In September, Dougal Haston and Doug Scott became the first British climbers to reach the summit of Mount Everest .

The Birmingham Six are wrongfully sentenced to life imprisonment and, Lord Lucan is found guilty of wilful murder of the nanny who was found dead at his wife's home.

Mt. Everest

FAMOUS PEOPLE WHO WERE BORN IN 1975

25th Feb: Naga Munchetty, television presenter
2nd May: David Beckham, footballer
27th May: Jamie Oliver, chef and TV personality
29th May: Melanie Brown, singer and Spice Girls member
4th Jun: Alex Wharf, English cricketer
26th Jul: Liz Truss, politician
5th Oct: Kate Winslet, actress
9th Nov: Gareth Malone, choir master
12th Nov: Katherine Grainger, rower

FAMOUS PEOPLE WHO DIED IN 1975

12th Feb: Bernard Knowles, Film director
14th Feb: P. G. Wodehouse, comic writer
3rd Mar: T. H. Parry-Williams, poet
3rd Apr: Mary Ure, actress
14th Apr: Michael Flanders, actor and songwriter
23rd Apr: William Hartnell, actor
20th May: Barbara Hepworth, sculptor
27th Nov: Ross McWhirter, co-founder of the Guinness Book of Records
29th Nov: Graham Hill, racing driver

LIFE IN 1975 - EASIER

```
X Z W R P F E S L N I W Y L O
T H A T C H E R K S R E W O T
R J K E E V E R E S T V J S H
U J T R W Q A L M O W X A D F
E M W A N A M O W K E B V E C
R G P G C R V R Y Z Q Y I D K
E U L R N I W I U G K H Z N N
D I F A S L O T S I P K C U A
R L S M C P Y T E I C O S O N
U T U O T F O S O R C I M F N
M Y P Y Q L O N D O N L F V Y
E Q U A L F J M J P S E T A G
D U V K Y R Q U Z W M M G E G
M O H M O U N T H N N B F V W
K S H Z G V R E X B Z K L O J
```

SOCIETY	EQUAL	FOUNDED	WOMAN
MARGARET	THATCHER	PISTOLS	TOWERS
MICROSOFT	EVEREST	GUILTY	NANNY
MURDER	MOUNT	LONDON	GATES

Born in 1975, you were one of 56.2 million people living in Britain and your life expectancy then was 72.5 years. There were 12.9 births per 1,000 population and you had a 1.5% chance of dying as an infant, a rapidly reduced chance as this figure in 1950 was almost 3.1%. The 11+ selective exam was almost totally phased out and comprehensive schools were the norm for most pupils from 11 years old.

In 1975, the basic rate of income tax was 35% of earnings. Strikes and industrial action continued to cause headaches for the government, and financial ruin for some companies who had to close.

The IRA continued their campaign of bombing, but the public resolutely went about their daily lives as normal and the government forged ahead with its programme of building new houses to accommodate an ever-increasing population. Councils too, caught up in the fever of new building, sometimes swept away parts of our architectural heritage to replace it with something less pleasing to the eye.

The NHS was starting to creak, though politicians were quick to deny there were any problems, and equally determined to phase out pay beds.

Chopper bikes were a status symbol for children; space hoppers were still 'cool' and there were video games and colour TV featuring Hong Kong Phooey, Fawlty Towers and Dr No was the first Bond film to be shown on British television; Queen releases Bohemian Rhapsody and The Wizard of Oz (1939 film) is shown on British television for the first time.

How Much Did It Cost?

The Average Pay	£3,380 (£65 pw)
The Average House	£10,000
Loaf of White Bread	15p
Pint of Milk	7p
Pint of Beer	28p
Gallon of Petrol	73p (15p a litre)
Newspapers	5p
To Post a letter in UK	7p
12mnths Road Tax	£40
TV Licence	B/W £8 Colour £18

On 3rd November the Forties Field was inaugurated by Her Majesty Queen Elizabeth at Aberdeen. It is the largest oilfield to be discovered so far in the British sector of the North Sea.

LIFE IN 1975 - HARDER

```
B U V N O I S I V E L E T B B D R C X C
X P G I E E M D Y L A M O R P X T I U B
O Y N G I A P M A C A H A A O T F A R W
A B O M B I N G C O E C E T P C H U K T
H N G J C R P O K M G N L E U R D D N N
D P B O W O M C I O W B F W L W W X Q Q
G E B W V M U A E X P E C T A N C Y H N
C N X A O E N N E N E S O Y T I S S X X
A X H D F G R C C N Y A M D I G T G Y G
O L A S G G I N S I L H P O O D R L L T
B T C I I X L E M G L P R S N G I A D E
E Y Q D N T H V E E W S E P G N K I I L
C V C Y L C I A H R N E H A E O E R P I
P L N H A L E R R E S T E H G I S T A Z
E C E D O B B Z B D U C N R A T L S R A
S K A B K P F N R U W U S Y T C H U Q B
X E M H O B P A P C O A I C I A I D P E
H Y A L M H Z E H E T Y V W R U G N X T
S F L M Q I E V R D B Y E Q E J L I H H
E D F Q W N O R R T P O E G H B N Z Y L
```

EXPECTANCY	POPULATION	RAPIDLY	REDUCED
COMPREHENSIVE	STRIKES	INDUSTRIAL	ACTION
HEADACHES	BOMBING	CAMPAIGN	COUNCILS
GOVERNMENT	ACCOMMODATE	HERITAGE	PHASE
CHOPPER	BOHEMIAN	SYMBOL	BRITISH
RHAPSODY	WIZARD	TELEVISION	ELIZABETH

JANUARY 1975

IN THE NEWS

WEEK 1

"Smaller Bags of Sugar" Pensioners and poorer families may struggle to pay the price rise of 28p for a 2lb bag of sugar. Metrication, will make available smaller half-kilo bags.

"Wasting Energy" Britain wastes more energy at home and in industry than other European countries. Scientists estimate that demand could be cut by a tenth in three years without lowering the standard of living.

WEEK 2

"No Longer Beatles" The Beatles & Co partnership was finally dissolved at a High Court hearing, eight years after it was first formed and five years after the group split up.

"Heating Controls" In a bid to conserve electricity, new Government regulations setting a maximum temperature of 20°C (68°F) in shops and offices and the use of daytime electricity for advertising signs took effect.

WEEK 3

"Ceasefire Ends" English cities are expected to bear the brunt of the Provisional IRA's renewed bombing campaign following the breakdown of the 25-day old ceasefire.

"Dangerous Games" A primary school playing field in Langney near Eastbourne, which was laid out on the site of an old refuse tip, has been closed by the council after toxic waste was discovered in water running through the field.

WEEK 4

"New Archbishop of Canterbury" During his enthronement in Canterbury Cathedral, the new Archbishop, Dr Coggan, took the oath on the priceless illuminated Gospels of St. Augustine which date from the 6th Century.

"Doctors to Strike" The Medical Practitioners' Union, which represents almost 5,000 doctors, has called for a 24-hour stoppage in a bid for improved pay.

HERE IN BRITAIN

"Disappointed Skiers"

Even in Speyside, which is normally bleak, the whole country is basking in the mildest January for fifty years. The slopes of Cairngorm, which by now should be covered in snow and skiers, remain black with earth and rocks.

One ski school has sent its instructors home and told them to return when the snow comes. By mid-January, between four and five thousand skiers would expect to be using the ski lift facilities on Cairngorm, but this year beginners are queuing up for lessons on an artificial slope in the Aviemore centre.

AROUND THE WORLD

"Tasman Bridge Disaster"

A large container ship collided with several pylons of the Tasman Bridge in Hobart, Tasmania, causing a large section of the bridge to collapse onto the ship and into the river below. As the collision occurred on the evening of 5th of January, which was a Sunday evening, there was less traffic on the bridge, but twelve people were killed.

Two drivers managed to stop at the edge, but not before their front wheels had dropped over the broken bridge deck. Fortunately, both drivers managed to ease themselves out of their cars to safety.

JANUARY 1975 - EASIER

```
A A C M B X N H Q Y Q I P N C
A R C H B I S H O P S P X Y O
F A M I L I E S S T L P O I N
I U V S E L T A E B A X K F T
J W S S U O R E G N A D M R
X Z X R E L L A M S Y S P F O
K I H R S D E K H A B Y S R L
N Q S G N I T S A W I P C P S
B K R C A N T E R B U R Y N C
S O O U E L Z E B S K I E R S
T F T G A M E S M Y G R E N E
R A C L O N G E R B E C T N L
I B O H E A T I N G O C W O X
K K D F N N W O Z C H Q R O B
E Y G T B G C E A S E F I R E
```

SMALLER	FAMILIES	WASTING	ENERGY
BEATLES	HEATING	CONTROLS	LONGER
CEASEFIRE	DANGEROUS	GAMES	ARCHBISHOP
CANTERBURY	DOCTORS	STRIKE	SKIERS

LIBERTY'S OF LONDON

Visitors to London are enjoying this year's mild January weather and thousands are visiting the famous Liberty store on Regent Street, both to view the building itself and to shop for the iconic Liberty print goods. The store was founded in 1875 by Arthur Lasenby Liberty, who borrowed £2,000 from his future father-in-law and bought the building. At first an importer of fabrics and objets d'arts, Arthur later collaborated with William Morris and began selling his own distinctive brand of fabrics in 1880.

The shop was completely redesigned in 1924 when a building firm was given a sum of £198,000 to create today's 'Mock Tudor' emporium. It was constructed from the timbers of two ancient ships, HMS Impregnable, built from 3,040 100-year-old oaks from the New Forest, and HMS Hindustan. More than 24,000 cubic feet of ships' timbers were used, including the decks, which became the shop flooring. Designed to feel like a home, each atrium was surrounded by smaller rooms, complete with fireplaces and furnishings made at the Liberty furniture workshops in Archway, London. Outside there is a gilded 4ft high, copper, weathervane of The Mayflower, which took pilgrims to the New World in 1620. The Liberty Clock on Kingly Street depicts St. George & The Dragon and tells us "*No minute gone comes ever back again, take heed and see ye nothing do in vain*" while inside on the old staircase, carved memorials remember the Liberty staff who died in World War II. There are Shields of Shakespeare and portraits of Henry VIII's six wives dotted about and carved wooden animals are hidden throughout the store. Sadly, Arthur Liberty never saw his dream realised, dying seven years before it opened but his statue stands at the Flower Shop entrance.

LIBERTY'S - HARDER

```
V T Y D E T C U R T S N O C R X M O Q D
E Y L E T E L P M O C C P O K L V W Q I
H F O R E S T Q H K O V C O X B L Q V S
E N J O Y I N G O L X D W K L G C H P T
J T D V L W R S L T E T I M B E R S G I
L J X R Y M Z A U H M G O M W F L M M N
J D G K C Y B F S T A I R C A S E A P C
P P E P W O X M D O X U R S L Z I I G T
X S P W R S V I S I T O R S C L F P C I
W S X A O I T K E Q R M P F L B O R L V
H G T Z C R V A K T U Z J I X R U U F E
Y E I O T N R A V I L R W Q T Y N J D J
D U N X O M I O R I G J E R C V D P B M
J I O D V S F O B Y B N A W K G E E I D
C V N A S D P E R O J I I G O T D F K R
B O A V Y M R A S X T O H D T L Z H E Y
L Q K L E T U U Q S I F C Z L H F G Q R
S R H F Y N S C I R B A F A Q I E Y Q P
J B U N A A N C I E N T A J L N U R A F
P S Z J T S H I E L D S M J T R Z B Y M
```

VISITORS	ENJOYING	LONDON	JANUARY
LIBERTY	REGENT	BUILDING	ICONIC
COLLABORATED	FOUNDED	BORROWED	WILLIAM
DISTINCTIVE	FABRICS	COMPLETELY	ANCIENT
EMPORIUM	CONSTRUCTED	TIMBERS	FOREST
MAYFLOWER	STAIRCASE	PORTRAITS	SHIELDS

11

IN THE NEWS

WEEK 1 **"Aid for Historic Churches"** The Government will donate £1m annually for the upkeep of historic churches that are still in use. Cathedrals will not receive the subsidy.

"Levy for Liability" Action on Smoking and Health (ASH) propose cigarette manufacturers should pay compensation for smoking related illnesses, to be funded by a 5p levy on each pack of cigarettes. Ash estimates there are 52,000 cigarette-associated deaths annually.

WEEK 2 **"Indefinite Ceasefire"** The IRA have declared an indefinite ceasefire in the United Kingdom. *"The organisation appears to be working towards a permanent cessation of violence,"* a spokesman said.

"Bumper Mailbag" Margaret Thatcher, the new Tory Leader, received many Valentine cards. One from an astrologer, predicted that she would become PM.

WEEK 3 **"Golden Eagles Back"** Ornithologists are guarding a pair of golden eagles which have returned to an eyrie in the Lake District. They are said to be England's only nesting pair of the birds of prey.

"Ferry Blockade" The Dover car ferry was turned back when 70 fishing vessels blocked Boulogne harbour, as French fisherman staged a 72-hour strike over low fish prices.

WEEK 4 **"Disappearing Gold"** Gold coins worth £150,000 are missing after 10 cartons each containing 500 coins, were loaded on to an aircraft in London, but only six arrived in Toronto. Canadian and British police are investigating.

"Prince on TV" As Patron of the Royal Anthropological Institute, Prince Charles is on location and involved in production of six anthropology programmes for the BBC.

HERE IN BRITAIN

"Pop Exhaustion"

The Edinburgh pop group, the Bay City Rollers, cancelled their European tour next month. Two members collapsed with nervous exhaustion, and the other three are expected to enter a nursing home this week.

One of the biggest selling acts in Britain, with their distinctive calf-length tartan trousers and tartan scarves. 'Rollermania' is on the rise, but fans are having difficulty keeping up with 'all things tartan' due to haberdashery shops all over the country running out of tartan fabric!

AROUND THE WORLD

"Nuclear Hell"

Hidden in Semipalatinsk, NE Kazakhstan, lies a nuclear hell, pockmarked with abandoned bunkers and craters, and an atomic lake known as 'The Polygon'. This was a primary testing site for Russian nuclear weapons, with facilities built using Gulag labour.

Over 400 nuclear bombs were detonated with no regard for the local people or environment. Russia falsely claimed the vast 18,000km² steppe was 'uninhabited', and details of the area were erased from maps for decades.

FEBRUARY 1975 - EASIER

```
C T D G C H U R C H E S L S X
I K B D E C A D E S W M A X H
M I N D E F I N I T E K R D I
O O S Y J R D B L O C K A D E
T I U Y G A B L I A M K X R B
A D V T J G O L D E N T Z V E
M G N I R A E P P A S I D C P
G J U L Y K D P G A Q D D Q R
N R D I E S H G R U B N I D E
Q A X B S A C A B U M P E R X
Y E F A X I J S E A G L E S U
Y L T I G X L E V Y B U R F P
G C W L R W E B W Z D P N U F
L U O U N O I T S U A H X E J
A N M H I S T O R I C Y P T V
```

HISTORIC	CHURCHES	LIABILITY	LEVY
INDEFINITE	BUMPER	MAILBAG	GOLDEN
DISAPPEARING	EAGLES	BLOCKADE	DECADES
EDINBURGH	NUCLEAR	EXHAUSTION	ATOMIC

WOMEN IN WESTMINSTER

Margaret Thatcher (top left), Nancy Astor (top right), Constance Markievicz (bottom right) and Florence Paton (bottom left).

On February 11th, 1975, Margaret Thatcher became the first woman to lead a political party in Britain after defeating both the current leader Edward Heath, and his preferred successor William Whitelaw.

Women have walked the corridors of Westminster in the pursuit of reform and women's' rights for many years. Some are remembered for their daring, others for breaking new ground. Suffragettes were asked to boycott the 1911 census because 'if they didn't count enough to have a vote, then 'neither shall they be counted'. Emily Wilding Davison chose to hide in a Westminster broom cupboard on that night to avoid appearing on any census form and was discovered by cleaners next morning.

Women aged 30 were given the vote in 1918 after World War I, in time for the General Election. The first woman to be elected to the House of Commons was Constance Markievicz, an Irish nationalist and revolutionary. A founding member of the Irish Citizen Army she took part in the Easter Rising of 1916, but as she was in Holloway Prison at the time of her election, she never took her seat. The first woman to actually take her seat in parliament, in 1919, was Nancy, Viscountess Astor, whose 2nd marriage gave her a title and a taste for politics. She represented Plymouth Sutton until 1945. Florence Paton she became the first woman to chair a debate on the Floor of the House of Commons in 1948. Margaret Bondfield was made the first female cabinet minister, and privy counsellor in 1929, and just after WWII became the first woman to preside over the whole House of Commons as Chairman of Committees, although she didn't occupy the Speaker's Chair. This privilege was not given to a woman until 1970 when Margaret Anderson became Deputy Speaker.

WOMEN - HARDER

```
D Y A W O L L O H D I A D X M Y X T M T
P N S D E N K Y L B E V T V R F O U Z V
S F C A K S K L F T I R V D O O C K R A
P R I R D G T R T S S W E U A I I E X F
R G T I D C Y M C H G I N B J D V S Z T
K U I N F N J O I N B D L Q M O C A O M
M D L G T H U R I N I O L A L E O P I W
R A O W T N E R S N S G Y U N W M S M E
O H P D T K A C G E A T T C F O M E F W
L P Q E A E D B O Y T I E I O I I Q R Q
L D S E P G M E D R O T I R U T T T Z B
E S P P K C A E J N R O E R O N T P A B
S S A J P N T W A D N I X G V D E P N N
N N A K P N W R P S L E D P A W E P E Q
U V Y O U O Y X O Q I E Q O E R S W M H
O R D O F E C N A T S N O C R U F L O B
C F C B B U C D O U W K L E C S O F W D
D I S C O V E R E D B L H U K F S W U B
Q D T H A T C H E R E D W A R D N F I S
M R O S S E C C U S P L Y M O U T H C C
```

THATCHER	EDWARD	SUCCESSOR	WOMEN
CORRIDORS	WESTMINSTER	REMEMBERED	DARING
SUFFRAGETTES	BOYCOTT	APPEARING	COUNTED
DISCOVERED	CONSTANCE	NATIONALIST	FOUNDING
REVOLUTIONARY	HOLLOWAY	PLYMOUTH	POLITICS
VISCOUNTESS	COUNSELLOR	COMMITTEES	SPEAKER

MARCH 1975

IN THE NEWS

WEEK 1   **"Refuse Tips Risk"** Uncollected refuse piling up in Glasgow city centre at the rate of a thousand tons a day, has become a serious health hazard as the strike is now 7 weeks old.

"Flood Prevention" Civil engineers can now design flood protection schemes, thanks to research work by a government team set up five years ago, to investigate ways of forecasting sporadic floods.

WEEK 2   **"Strike Costs Jobs"** British Leyland strikers may face redundancy when the strike ends. The company has lost a £2m contract from Korea.

"Airlines Want More Concordes" British and French aircraft industries are pressing for six additional Concorde supersonic airliners to be built.

WEEK 3   **"Rush to Beat the Post"** The Post Office handled piles of extra mail as people rushed to beat the newly introduced 7p first-class letter postage rate.

"Teacher Redundancies" Richmond's Council is to cut £1m from the education budget making 200 teachers redundant, after talks with national teachers unions.

WEEK 4   **"Sell by Dates"** Legislation will require food processors and shopkeepers to show, on packets of pre-packed foods, the dates by which they should be sold. White sugar, fresh, fruit and vegetables, and frozen products are exempt.

"North Wind Doth Blow" An Arctic air stream swept across the country this Easter weekend causing Heathrow airport to close for two hours to clear the snow.

HERE IN BRITAIN

"Trudeau in Town"

Mr Pierre Trudeau, the Canadian Prime Minister, inspected a guard of honour of the Honourable Artillery Company at Guildhall before he received the Freedom of the City of London, one of the oldest surviving traditional ceremonies still in existence, and an honour which is only open to Commonwealth and British citizens.

Traditionally but apocryphally associated with freemen rights, include the right to drive sheep and cattle over London Bridge and carry a naked sword in public.

AROUND THE WORLD

"Doctor Yellow"

'Doctor Yellow' is the nickname for high-speed diagnostic trains that are used on the Bullet train lines in Japan. They have a distinctive yellow livery giving rise to the name and are fitted with electronic equipment to monitor the condition of the track and overhead cables.

Line inspections are carried out regularly at full speed, up to 270 km/h or 168 mph but because the schedule for this train is not publicised, witnessing a Doctor Yellow in operation is by pure chance. As a result, seeing one is believed to bring the viewer good luck.

MARCH 1975 - EASIER

```
A E A F L O O D N U H C V G Y
I D X M N O D N O L G R O P M
R U T G U H B E I Z S E O R Y
L C M V A J Y K T Q K K E O B
I A B I E F R E N C H G G C I
N T V Q D G S D E C J F D E B
E I Z B U E N T V J D T I S Z
B O G Z R S X Q E K R E R S R
Z N M N T H X F R G U C B O J
R E T S I N I M P Q O Y G R P
P S E I C N A D N U D E R S T
U S Z Z H F R E E M A N Q X Y
K L G P R E F U S E S E T A D
X H D E T A I C O S S A C C J
T E A C H E R T V A K W F W H
```

REFUSE   FLOOD   PREVENTION   AIRLINE

FRENCH   TEACHER   REDUNDANCIES   EDUCATION

DATES   PROCESSORS   TRUDEAU   MINISTER

ASSOCIATED   FREEMAN   LONDON   BRIDGE

OUR DEBT TO THE RNLI

Nine Lifeboat Stations mark 150 years' service this year; Appledore, Courtmacsherry, Cromer, Dun Laoghaire, Hartlepool, Howth, Newcastle Co. Down, Padstow and Skegness. And yet perhaps because lifeboatmen are characteristically modest about their work, perhaps because the service they perform makes no financial demands on the ratepayer or taxpayer, many people seem unaware of the hundreds of lives they save each year and the risks they undergo. The lifeboat is expected to be at hand when needed, like the police car, the fire engine or the ambulance. The lifeboat is expected to be on hand when needed, like police cars, fire engines or ambulances. That the Royal National Life-boat Institution is supported entirely by voluntary subscriptions probably only occurs to the average person for a few moments a year when he sees a collection box or a poster appealing for funds.

Yet in coastal towns and villages the threat of disaster at sea is more imminent, the lifeboat service is more familiar and volunteers to man the boats continue to come forward amidst the changing nature of the services they have been called on to perform in recent years. The decline of the fishing industry in many parts of the country has been accompanied by a phenomenal increase in the number of pleasure-boat owners, out in force during the main holiday months of July, August and September.

As an official put it, the institution's charter is to rescue people from the sea without distinction between nationalities or circumstances and this includes 'bloody fools' as much as those who are victims of an Act of God. A glance at the accounts of rescues in the institution's quarterly journal will convince both the unfortunate and the foolish how great is their debt to those who uncomplainingly risk their lives to save others.

THE RNLI - HARDER

```
H K E Y R S E C N A T S M U C R I C Y A
S T X T G J W R E T S A S I D C X F E M
I V W N A T I O N A L I T I E S U O C B
L Y V N O S N O I T P I R C S B U S N U
O G Z N B F J A C F E G S Z W W P Q I L
O O W F E H A F Z U Z L Q Q S L O T V A
F B W L H N U M J A Z V T U W X L H N N
T J V E L N I I I L V R O S J J I G O C
E M F L D T D G N L A I A L A C C C C E
V I O E S F A K N S I I C T U C E X F P
R K R D Q E I O O E T A C T E N W A U R
F G L B E L P S B C E I R N I P T E U M
O O A F A S U T H E S R T B A M A A N N
R H N D H T T T E I F N I U J N S Y R W
U D O D Q A W Q L M N I M F T N I Z E Y
M T I N M T J P C Q B G L V G I S F U R
T X T F Z I J K Q U M E A L H Y O K G K
T D A T T O O A S U G Y R L A T N N E Q
R U N R F N F G Q T P Q B K W K T Q E F
U M M J P S G J B B W D S E U C S E R Q
```

LIFEBOAT	STATIONS	NEWCASTLE	MODEST
FINANCIAL	RATEPAYER	AMBULANCE	UNDERGO
FIRE ENGINE	NATIONAL	SUBSCRIPTIONS	POLICE
INSTITUTION	VOLUNTARY	FAMILIAR	DISASTER
NATIONALITIES	SEPTEMBER	FISHING	VICTIMS
CIRCUMSTANCES	RESCUES	FOOLISH	CONVINCE

APRIL 1975

IN THE NEWS

WEEK 1   **"Fish Prices Up"** Some retail fish prices have risen by half because of the inshore fishermen's blockade of English and Scottish ports. Varieties such as whiting, herring and mackerel may soon become scarce.

"Resistance to Diets" Scientists have proved that prolonged dieting can lead to a drop in the body's need for food meaning that a standard reducing diet no longer has any effect.

WEEK 2   **"Cairngorms Blizzard"** Severe blizzards swept the Cairngorms and holidaymakers were kept from the ski slopes by high winds and heavy snow.

"Live Exports" The Ministry of Agriculture is to tighten regulations in the live export of animals, due to allegations of cruelty to sheep exported to France.

WEEK 3   **"A New Star"** A new type of star has been discovered by astronomers from universities in London and Birmingham. It was discovered using the British satellite known as 'Ariel-S'.

"Fighting Water Pollution" Awards for Industry have been given to five British and two international companies for schemes to reduce water pollution. The gold medal was won by the Scottish Distillers Company.

WEEK 4   **"Thanksgiving Service"** The Queen attended a service of thanksgiving on St. George's Day with members of the Royal Family, at St George's Chapel, Windsor, to celebrate the 500th Anniversary of its construction.

"High Price to Pay" The annual cost of running the average family car has risen by nearly £240 in the past year, which for many is more than the house mortgage repayments.

HERE IN BRITAIN

"Rough, Tough, Budget"

Denis Healey posed for photographers on the steps of No.11 Downing Street, with the red leather dispatch box. He delivered a "rough, tough" Spring budget, raising taxes, cutting spending, and higher duty on alcohol, cigarettes and bingo.

The leader of the opposition, Margaret Thatcher, called it a genuine socialist budget, 'equal shares of misery for all'. A suspicious object on a Foreign Office windowsill overlooking Downing Street, was found by police to be someone's packed lunch!

AROUND THE WORLD

"Microsoft Born"

'Popular Electronics' ran a feature on the Altair 8800 microcomputer which inspired childhood friends Bill Gates and Paul Allen to set up a business using their skills in computer programming.

They submitted to the computer company MITS, that they could program a BASIC (Beginners' All-purpose Symbolic Instruction Code) interpreter for the Altair 8800 which they successfully demonstrated. Gates and Allen then established their own company, Microsoft.

APRIL 1975 - EASIER

```
Q S V M P O L L U T I O N F Y
M C F I G H T I N G I R J R O
R I E K O K U K G S O E N G O
E N R V N J A Z N N R T D O M
S O O E A W Q R I C K A E O I
I R X G U K K B V N Y W X M C
S T S T E I D G I Q S J L A R
T C G W K C P N G U T Y T C O
A E S C O T T I S H R P V K S
N L H G U O R N K W O R A E O
C E V G P N X W N V P O V R F
E C P R U R M O A P X G I E T
B L I Z Z A R D H S E R R L W
P K M P C I S H T B N A V X F
T E G D U B J B I B G M S N Y
```

MACKEREL	SCOTTISH	RESISTANCE	DIETS
BLIZZARD	EXPORTS	FIGHTING	WATER
POLLUTION	THANKSGIVING	ROUGH	BUDGET
DOWNING	MICROSOFT	ELECTRONICS	PROGRAM

EAGLE-BRITAIN'S NATIONAL STRIP CARTOON WEEKLY

LIVING WITH EAGLES

PRIEST TO PUBLISHER THE LIFE AND TIMES OF MARCUS MORRIS

Sally Morris and Jan Hallwood

25 years ago this month, the most famous of Marcus Morris's publications, 'The Eagle' comic went on sale. Born in Preston, Lancashire the son of a clergyman, Morris became an Anglican Priest in 1940 and from the beginning, he published Christian magazines for his younger parishioners, illustrated by Frank Hampson. He was part of a group of editors who formed the Society of Christian Publicity, and wrote an article entitled "Comics that bring Horror into the Nursery", decrying the violence of American crime and horror comics. He was impressed by the high standard of artwork but disgusted by their content. Realising a market existed for a children's comic featuring cartoon action stories but conveying Christian standards and morals, he and Hampson produced The Eagle.

The comic was enormously successful, the first issue selling 900,000 copies. The full colour cover featured the iconic *"Dan Dare, Pilot of The Future"*, created by Hampson, which was the UK's first science-fiction comic strip of any significance. Other popular stories included *"Riders of the Range"* and *"PC. 49"*. Eagle also contained news, sport sections, and educational cutaway diagrams of sophisticated machinery, the first of which, detailed the inner workings of the British Rail 18000 locomotive.

A member's club was created, and a range of related merchandise licensed for sale. The comic was heavily publicised before its release; copies were mailed direct to several hundred thousand people who worked with children, and a "Hunt the Eagle" scheme was launched, whereby large papier-mâché golden eagles were set on top of several Humber Hawk cars, and toured across Britain. Those who spotted an eagle were offered tokens worth 3d which could be exchanged for a free copy.

```
Q O E K C E Y A Z S S K B X U P L W R S
N Y J R B G Q I D S S U M M F K I A Q Y
V R T R I R F A A O K A C V C O M I C S
E I F E F H Y N X U W A L C S O A R A K
F E O X I J S C N D U M A E E G G M E M
Y X N L M C I A E Q C C L U V S D L K C
T C E S E W O C C X Y L P E I F S C P X
I H D N H N R S D N I P H G T Z S F S M
C A L P X Y C E I N A T X A O C K X U J
I N O W I O R E G K F L S C M D M J K L
L G G N E E N S Q Y I F H M O R S X B I
B E G Q F R W F L E W R L A C R K Z I N
U D F F O D A S W L I E I T O V M L S A
P K O R O M U C N S T S L T L N Y M I M
E C R D O O K E T U X S I G B L B T R Y
H O P U M L J I F G R D U C A I U I R G
H G S R G J A R H I E S S C A E A T O R
S D O G V N P A Z T O U E T R G E N M E
S N M E R C H A N D I S E R T A U H Q L
E E N T I T L E D Q E V C U Y D M I T C
```

FAMOUS	MARCUS	THE EAGLE	LANCASHIRE
CLERGYMAN	MORRIS	EDITORS	SOCIETY
CHRISTIAN	PUBLICITY	ENTITLED	DECRYING
VIOLENCE	NURSERY	COMICS	HORROR
ENORMOUSLY	SUCCESSFUL	SELLING	LOCOMOTIVE
MERCHANDISE	GOLDEN	OFFERED	EXCHANGED

MAY 1975

IN THE NEWS

WEEK 1   **"Wild Birds Protest"** 600,000 wild birds are imported into Britain annually. The RSPB criticises the conditions in which they are trapped and is calling for a Government ban.

"New Paper for Scotland" The first edition of the Scottish Daily News has rolled off the press in Glasgow, watched by the Secretary of State for Industry, and Robert Maxwell.

WEEK 2   **"Channel Island Celebrations"** An exhibition opened at the Imperial War Museum to celebrate the thirtieth anniversary of the Islands' liberation from German occupation.

"Old Attitude" The agriculture minister has criticised those who believe that Britain can find adequate and cheap food supplies outside the EEC. The idea that Commonwealth countries would *'queue up to meet our needs if we left the Community'* revealed *'an outmoded attitude.'*

WEEK 3   **"Blood Trade"** The World Health Organization has expressed concern over the extensive trade in human blood, which is sold by the poor in underdeveloped countries for export.

"Radio 1 "Roadshow Disaster" 39 people received hospital treatment following a crush of fans at the Radio One Road Show. The Bay City Rollers left without performing.

WEEK 4   **"Medical Loss Causing Concern"** In the past year 284 hospital consultants and 40 senior registrars have emigrated. Most leave for Canada, with others going to America, Australia, New Zealand and Saudi Arabia.

"Coach Crash" A coach crashed through the side of Dibble's Bridge in Yorkshire, dropping 25ft to the river below. The accident happened just outside Hebden Bridge, on the Grassington Road. 32 people were killed and 14 seriously injured.

HERE IN BRITAIN
"Whittington Walks"

A group of London mayors, and mayoresses, dressed in traditional ceremonial attire, including fur-trimmed red cloaks, black hats and heavy gold chains, began their annual five-mile charity walk from Highgate Hill at the statue of Dick Whittington and his cat to the Mansion House.
This commemorates the 'turning again' of Dick Whittington before he became Lord Mayor of London. The London Pearly Kings' and Queens' Society, one of London's oldest charities, accompanied the councillors.

AROUND THE WORLD
"Giant Hailstones in Tennessee"

During a recent storm, hail stones as large as tennis balls hit Wernerville, TN. Farmers affected by the hail are now evaluating the extent of damage to their crops and determining if replanting will be necessary. The whole state is prone to thunderstorms, tornadoes, and hurricanes.

When hail reaches 2 inches or larger in diameter, it is classed as 'Significant Severe Hail' which coupled with winds of 75 mph or higher, can cause considerable damage.

MAY 1975 - EASIER

```
O C E L E B R A T I O N S W H
E C D X D I D K D L G C R S R
D L E G U H W I N O M P E X S
A I S H T D S R A N J G P Y O
M T S A I Z G O L D T F A X C
A U E A T Q N A T O Q L P X I
G U R I T A I D O N F E G M E
E F P T A B K S C A L C D Y T
C T X U A Z E H S E P Y J K Y
Y Q E Z S E N O T S L I A H G
L P L J M E B W C F V T V F G
R E L A I N O M E R E C U P Q
A D P A P D D R E T E M A I D
E A R K W I L A C I D E M F I
P O T M F T S E T O R P T J I
```

PROTEST	SCOTLAND	CELEBRATIONS	PAPER
ATTITUDE	EXPRESSED	ROADSHOW	MEDICAL
LONDON	CEREMONIAL	PEARLY	KINGS
SOCIETY	HAILSTONES	DAMAGE	DIAMETER

THE FALL OF SAIGON

SURRENDER!

Saigon Yields Unconditionally; End Comes Only Hours After Last Americans Fly Out

On the 30th April, South Vietnamese President Duong Van Minh announced an unconditional surrender, asking his forces to lay down their arms. In a radio address to the Vietcong he said, "*We are here to hand over to you the power in order to avoid bloodshed,*" and appealed to them to halt all hostilities, bringing 35 years of fighting in South Vietnam to an end.

Swarms of helicopters lifted thousands of Americans and Vietnamese military and civilian personnel from Saigon in the final withdrawal from Vietnam. Twenty years of United States involvement ended in scenes of chaos as weeping Vietnamese pleaded for places in evacuation convoys and tried to force their way into the American Embassy. American Marine and civilian helicopters, flying in groups of three, plucked evacuees from the top of the embassy building and ledges of blocks of flats. The evacuation began after a Vietcong demand, agreed to by President Duong Van Minh, that all Americans leave the country within 24 hours, the withdrawal of the United States Seventh Fleet from Vietnam waters and the disarming of Saigon's army and police.

Meanwhile in the streets, looting broke out - two policemen were seen putting their weapons into a chest of drawers to be able to cart it away more easily, while small boys struggled to carry away armchairs.Helicopters were ditched wholesale into the sea in the frantic evacuation. In the first 90 minutes of the operation, 14 helicopters carrying among others, Air Vice-Marshal Nguyen Cao Ky, the former vice-president, landed on the small helicopter pad on the back of the command ship Blue Ridge, and were then dumped, after discharging their passengers, into the sea to make room for more, while rescue boats sped around the ship to fish out the helicopter pilots.

SAIGON - HARDER

```
Y R W A M U U E P F V I E T N A M E S E
B K S Q X N K L R X P R E S I D E N T E
Y D M L G Z D E L A S E L O H W H Q W A
L H R I D N Z S T O L I P J K Q E B J K
A C N A I L I V I C U L Y S X A L B S R
W G S D N A S U O H T D U U O S I Y H D
A C G H O S T I L I T I E S X U C W O E
R D N I I P D A P Q F I C H N R O G P H
D T I E O T O X A Y M O R C E R P N P S
H D G W S K J S K X Q C O G E E T I N D
T D R F P F E U N M P N I L C N E M U O
I K A I L A B C X A D Y O I O D R R J O
W I H G Y Y S V I I C O S P S E S A W L
K Y C H C R Z S T L T I E S I R C S E B
D L S T S V E I E I O R R J A F T I A W
O I I I N A O S N N A P H E E B T D P M
J R D N J N I G C T G P X R M P M Y O A
T S F G A A P G I U H E D I A A R E N R
Y E Z L S Q N O O P E T R X F C Z E S D
O O J V S W N A L N Q A L S G U S I U X
```

SURRENDER	AMERICANS	VIETNAMESE	PRESIDENT
UNCONDITIONAL	BLOODSHED	HOSTILITIES	FIGHTING
HELICOPTERS	THOUSANDS	SAIGON	CIVILIAN
WITHDRAWAL	EMBASSY	DISARMING	POLICE
LOOTING	WEAPONS	WHOLESALE	RESCUE
OPERATION	PASSENGERS	DISCHARGING	PILOTS

JUNE 1975

IN THE NEWS

WEEK 1 **"Aspro Jobs Lost"** 120 members of the staff at Slough's Aspro-Nicholas research plant are being made redundant following the company's decision to relocate to Paris.

"Snowdon Wearing Away" Snowdon is being eroded by the vast number of visitors. It has been recommended that the whole area should be managed by a special committee.

WEEK 2 **"County Closes School"** Durham County Council have challenged the NUT advice to teachers not to teach disruptive pupils, by closing a 1,000-pupil school where staff are following the Union's advice.

"Mine Explosion" The Coal Board closed the faces at Houghton Main colliery in South Yorkshire, where an explosion has killed five men. The Energy Secretary reminded people of the dangerous price of providing coal.

WEEK 3 **"Lord Lucan Accused"** Lady Lucan identified her husband as her assailant who tried to strangle her in their home on the night their children's nursemaid was found dead.

"Beagles Stolen" Two beagles used in experiments with cigarettes, have been stolen by Animal Rights activists, who informed the press *"One of the dogs coughed and wheezed like a human being who has smoked for 30 years"*

WEEK 4 **"Save The Whales"** Delegates of The International Whaling Council met in London to set limits on the hunting of whales. Peter Scott warned whales are on the brink of extinction.

"County Hospital – A Medical Slum" Doctors at the Royal Hampshire County Hospital in Winchester complained in an open letter of *'the medically dangerous conditions of a 19th century Building'* describing it as a medical slum.

HERE IN BRITAIN

"Snow Falls on London"

This week saw the first snow and sleet to fall across all parts of the country in summer since 1888. An inch of snow covered the cricket pitch at Buxton and snowflakes fell briefly on Lord's cricket ground in London.

Arctic winds swept across the UK with 3.3C recorded in Scotland, more like the depths of winter than early summer. Sleet was reported as far south as Portsmouth. It melted quickly across the South but lingered on the ground for days in parts of Scotland.

AROUND THE WORLD

"Open-Rear Buses in Paris"

This summer it will be possible to ride on the open rear platform of a Paris bus again, after the practice was abolished in early 1971. The new, old-style buses are being re-introduced to please both Parisians and tourists.

There will be one difference - the chains which used to let the adventurous leap on and off the rear platform have gone. Access will now be only through the bus, which, considering the speed and volume of Paris traffic, is probably a wise safety precaution.

JUNE 1975 - EASIER

```
S N A I S I R A P T P T W A B
E F S R Z I P M Y T E F A S E
W H A L E S X S P Z O W W F A
R P Z J V A W I R K S J E C G
G T N A D N U D E R G D A N L
O K H F V E F L C M S B R C E
I J O J I K H X A E Q B I O S
K S S E S S C P U D P P N L P
V F P X I X R O T I C V G L I
U M I X T U A U I C I W H I P
Q C T Z O W E G O A T O F E R
K V A R R E S T N L C N T R B
N H L H S W E Y M B R S B Y K
L O O H C S R Y J Q A R C G Z
N P P X D Q Y R A T E R C E S
```

RESEARCH	REDUNDANT	WEARING	VISITORS
SCHOOL	COLLIERY	SECRETARY	BEAGLES
WHALES	HOSPITAL	MEDICAL	SNOW
ARCTIC	PARISIANS	PRECAUTION	SAFETY

NATIONAL GARDEN SCHEME

The National Garden Scheme is a charity which raises millions of pounds each year for nursing and health charities, community gardens, and other causes by giving visitors unique access to many exceptional private gardens in the UK. One special garden which opened for just one day in June is Choumert Square. Although it is called 'Square', it is actually a narrow lane-way of 46 tiny cottages and tiny gardens of a secret Southwark street. They have evolved over some 40 years, triggered initially by a few residents' passion for gardening that infused the enthusiasm of others, and they are now a famous London landmark.

The Square was named after the Frenchman, George Choumert who owned the land, and in the 19th Century, had these artisan cottages built. The 1891 Census lists the various occupations of the 106 residents, from bricklayer, dressmaker, and bookbinder, to carpenter, pastry cook and steam engine fitter.

Today the properties are classed as either single occupancy or for a couple, but in the same 1891 census one little house on the North side was home to at least 6 people. Back then, Choumert Square was known to locals as Cut-Throat Lane, so it was obviously far less salubrious than today. Plants seem to thrive in the soil here as it is very rich from past generations when the land was used for market gardening. Today, the Square gardens demonstrate how gardening can unite a community. The street divides into a sunny side and a shady side, which is reflected in the planting. A wide variety of roses provide colour for much of the year against a backdrop of a mixture of trees including birch, willow, and eucalyptus whilst pots are filled with a colourful array of perennial border plants and annuals.

NATIONAL GARDEN - HARDER

```
N E O R R K T E M E H C S Q B E G A E D
P E W C E X C E P T I O N A L R E E K R
H I E N T H U S I A S M A R E A N K V E
C P R I V A T E T J N O J Y L U E O H S
N U R S I N G L L H F C A W R Q R T G S
O V W Q E R A R Q A H L O P X S A L G M
T S C E N S U S G A K R R M P C T R W A
P R T W L O Z Y R C N C X D M O I E D K
E S J I W I T I I K A D B C P U O D M E
R N P W N V T R S L A N O I T A N N X R
E V L D L Y B N N O I S S A P Q S I E I
N S U A V N E W G S G D Z K R I K B T O
N N M O N D Q E S N H T L A E H U K M Y
I O P F R D K W I F K A Z L E N C O I M
A I K A P Q M T V J L O Q T I U G O R K
L L G O E K N A O Q X V O Q M U A B A X
J L G N O A L D R P X U U M I V I I I W
Z I S X L T V M Z K W E F G F A Y S S G
S M H P N G I C C P S O P W Z F F C E O
H I N O T I N C O T T A G E S N M E S S
```

NATIONAL	**RAISES**	**SCHEME**	**CHARITY**
MILLIONS	**NURSING**	**HEALTH**	**COMMUNITY**
GARDENS	**UNIQUE**	**EXCEPTIONAL**	**PRIVATE**
COTTAGES	**PASSION**	**ENTHUSIASM**	**LANDMARK**
SQUARE	**BRICKLAYER**	**DRESSMAKER**	**BOOKBINDER**
CENSUS	**GENERATIONS**	**PLANTING**	**PERENNIAL**

JULY 1975

IN THE NEWS

WEEK 1   **"Below the Mark"** 60% of the doctors from overseas failed the General Medical Council's first compulsory language and medical competence tests.

"Magna Carta on Loan" For the bicentennial celebrations of American independence, this year, the British Library is to lend to the United States Congress, one of its four original copies of the Magna Carta.

WEEK 2   **"Leaving School Early"** Proposals have been made to allow all pupils who are 16 to leave school at the spring Bank holiday instead of waiting until the end of the summer term.

"Roadside Savings" To save up to £1m, the Department of the Environment will stop cutting grass on motorways and trunk roads, except if vegetation impedes visibility.

WEEK 3   **"Court Will Sit Late"** The court at Bow Street, will be kept open until late for the arrival from Australia of the runaway MP John Stonehouse, and secretary, Sheila Buckley, to face charges of fraud, theft and conspiracy.

"Butter Production Stopped" An increasing shortage of milk due to poor grass growth, and increased slaughter of dairy cattle, has led the Milk Marketing Board to call for a halt to production of butter for the foreseeable future.

WEEK 4   **"Road Maintenance Cuts"** Spending on trunk road maintenance will be cut by 20% by surface dressings rather than resurfacing, less footpath repairs and grass cutting.

"BBC Quits India" The BBC has suspended its news operations in India, as the new Indian censorship regulations are *'unacceptable'*, and would prevent giving *'a fair and authentic picture of events'* there. India. Mark Tully, the correspondent, has been withdrawn.

HERE IN BRITAIN

"Chawton Festival"

The summer fete was celebrated at the village of Chawton in Hampshire, the home of Jane Austen. Schoolchildren danced round the maypole and the church where Jane's mother and sister are buried, was decorated with flowers.
Pilgrims inspected Jane's house and the oak she planted and the views she described, walking the paths she trod. She would have been moved and amused by the grand festivities with which her village is celebrating the two hundredth anniversary of her birth.

AROUND THE WORLD

"Noonday Gun Continues"

The historic noonday gun on Hong Kong's waterfront has finally been cleared of guilt in a charge of noise pollution brought by a mother in claiming that the blast frightened her child.

Her complaint caused much indignation in the Hong Kong Club and among older residents, who respect the gun as one of the colony's ancient traditions. In the words of Noel Coward's famous song "In Hong Kong they strike a gong and fire off a midday gun, but mad dogs and Englishmen go out in the noonday sun."

JULY 1975 - EASIER

```
R Q N W J Z F E R E M M U S C
W M Z K C I G O Y D C J M O I
E T Y J Q H I S T O R I C B L
B C H D O C T O R S Q M K K A
I M A I N T E N A N C E J C N
C G V R E B P X L O B D A O G
E X S P R M R Y O I X I N M U
N I M A I Q O P O T C C C P A
T Q I J H U D I H A F A Y U G
E J R R S I U K C R N L A L E
N T G E P T C U S B G L D S Q
N F L T M S T J V E H S N O T
I X I T A I I F X L J J O R J
A S P U H Y O O C E N J O Y O
L Y U B G N N F M C V Z N F U
```

DOCTORS	MEDICAL	COMPULSORY	LANGUAGE
SCHOOL	CELEBRATIONS	BICENTENNIAL	SUMMER
BUTTER	PRODUCTION	MAINTENANCE	QUITS
HAMPSHIRE	PILGRIMS	NOONDAY	HISTORIC

St Swithun's Day

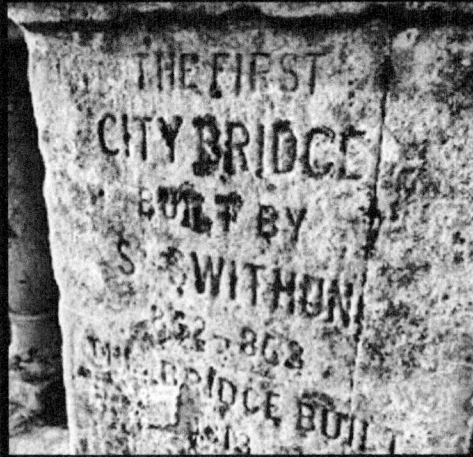

St. Swithun was an Anglo-Saxon bishop of Winchester in the 9th century. Noted for humility, he was popular with the people. On his deathbed Swithin begged to be buried outside the north wall of his cathedral, unlike other religious nobility who were buried close to the altar. He wanted to be where passers-by walked, and rain fell on it. In 971 AD, the restoration and enlargement of the building was completed, and Swithin was adopted as the cathedral's patron saint. To mark the occasion, Swithun's body was dug up and re-interred on 15th July, with much ceremony, in the new cathedral behind the altar.

Numerous miracles were reported following the move. The two most famous 'miracles' are those of the Winchester egg-seller, and Queen Emma's ordeal. A woman was going to sell a basket of eggs at market. They were snatched by some workmen as a prank and got broken. In tears she prayed to St Swithun, and the eggs were 'miraculously' restored. Queen Emma, the mother of Edward the Confessor, was accused of having an affair, and to prove her innocence had to walk on red hot ploughshares. The night before her ordeal she prayed to St Swithun, and the next day was able to walk on the hot metal without injury.

According to tradition, if it rains on Saint Swithun's bridge, opposite Winchester Water Mill, on 15th July, it will rain for forty days. There is a scientific basis for this, which is that around mid-July, the jet stream settles into a pattern which holds reasonably steady until the end of August. When it lies north of Britain, continental high pressure moves in; but when it lies across or south of Britain, cooler and wetter Atlantic weather systems predominate.

St Swithun's - Harder

```
T C V K Z L A R D E H T A C Y P E Y E K
Y E C S R H P D E H C T A N S T R N O B
T I Q P R O S S E F N O C R F U L D A U
I W D E B H T A E D T R Q Y J A E N I R
L R N O I T I D A R T J M N R R G P R I
I K E J B O V P O B N V I G O L N Q E E
M A X T R M W H B H C B E S O N U N S D
U S L M S S N Q N I Y M T S L X H Y T Y
H B E M D E N S C D E R A F G D T B O F
V M W R W A H J C N O X D E R R I S R Q
M R Q A A H A C T I O G J E M A W R A D
P K I L X H O L N N E A S V T W S E T H
P T I U K F S Y T I V N T O D D T S I R
Q C N P C Q F H Y A W H T E A E S S O C
A X O O X T O V G M R M C I P B U A N Z
X S C P N I Y O M U E B L V F Q V P N T
G R E L L E S G G E O U P U T I Y G P A
M J N U M E R O U S P L S D Z U C Y P H
R S E L C A R I M O H S P K X D J Q D U
F U Q O T W O R K M E N B R I T A I N D
```

ST SWITHUN	ANGLO-SAXON	WINCHESTER	HUMILITY
POPULAR	DEATHBED	CATHEDRAL	BURIED
PASSERS-BY	RESTORATION	ENLARGEMENT	ALTAR
NUMEROUS	MIRACLES	EGG-SELLER	SNATCHED
WORKMEN	EDWARD	CONFESSOR	INJURY
PLOUGHSHARES	TRADITION	SCIENTIFIC	BRITAIN

AUGUST 1975

IN THE NEWS

WEEK 1 **"Rising Health Costs"** The DHSS report that the cost of prescriptions issued by doctors rose by £40m last year, with 10 million more being issued.

"Reluctant Parenting" The Office of Population Censuses and Surveys has confirmed that the trend for couples to put off having children due to the uncertain and volatile current economic situation, is likely to continue.

WEEK 2 **"Pledge to End Tied Cottages"** The Government is to abolish tied cottages on farms and give 70,000 farm workers the protection of the Rent Acts against eviction.

"Not Amused" Mary Whitehouse of the National Viewers and Listeners' Association, criticised Betty Ford, wife of the US President, for saying, *'that in general premarital relations 'with the right partner' might reduce the divorce rate'.*

WEEK 3 **"High Price of Violence"** The cost of policing fan violence outside football grounds cost the general public £750,000 last year, and may well exceed £1m this season.

"Smallpox Scare" As the World Health Organisation approaches the end of its worldwide smallpox eradication campaign, a 12-year-old British boy with suspected smallpox was admitted to a hospital in Lancashire for tests.

WEEK 4 **"Asleep at The Wheel"** A Swedish 30ft yacht was found by the Torbay lifeboat, drifting through Channel shipping lanes, with the lone crew member of the vessel sound asleep. He was sailing from the West Indies to Sweden.

"Pupil's Choice" The Scottish Council of the Labour Party's report on school truancy, suggests pupils should choose their own teachers. It stated that truants chose specific times to stay away, to avoid subjects and teachers they disliked.

HERE IN BRITAIN

"Outlook Changeable"

New BBC TV weather symbols are to be introduced to give viewers a clearer understanding after complaints that triangles (representing showers) and dots (rain) are not sufficiently intelligible.

The new system uses symbols, utilising one 'cloud', shaped like a cottage loaf, black for those threatening rain and white for others. From it will emerge blue teardrops (rain), yellow flashes (lightning) or yellow rays to illustrate that every cloud has a silver lining. Fog, however, will not have a symbol, it remains as FOG.

AROUND THE WORLD

"Kissinger Upstaged"

Elizabeth Taylor and Richard Burton arrived in Tel Aviv to make a film in Jerusalem and stole the show from the American Secretary of State, Dr Henry Kissinger.

Before they arrived at the King David I Hotel, whose historic guests have included Sir Winston Churchill and King Farouk, the star guest, Dr Kissinger, and his party had taken over the entire sixth floor. However once the Burtons were ensconced in rooms 228, 229 and 230, the talk was of nothing else!

AUGUST 1975 - EASIER

```
O T R U A N C Y D H A V Z A S
K H L F C N U P S T A G E D S
C J Q R E L U C T A N T X W M
C V I O L E N C E G V W Q X A
B J K E W E A T H E R Y Q B L
G N I T N E R A P Q I T P C L
A S L E E P C J M I P P X I P
G L O W M R P Q L R V S Q R O
D N F R E G N I S S I K N O X
E I R E L B A E G N A H C T Y
S E A P E G D E L P E H V S V
U G L Y H T L A E H D G Y I Z
M A W W E A F E K P R L F H O
A S L O B M Y S A J O V L E E
T N O T S N I W B Z K X D X C
```

HEALTH	RELUCTANT	PARENTING	PLEDGE
AMUSED	VIOLENCE	SMALLPOX	ASLEEP
TRUANCY	CHANGEABLE	SYMBOLS	WEATHER
KISSINGER	UPSTAGED	HISTORIC	WINSTON

EDINBURGH FRINGE FESTIVAL

EDINBURGH
INTERNATIONAL
FESTIVAL 24 AUGUST - 13 SEPTEMBER 1975

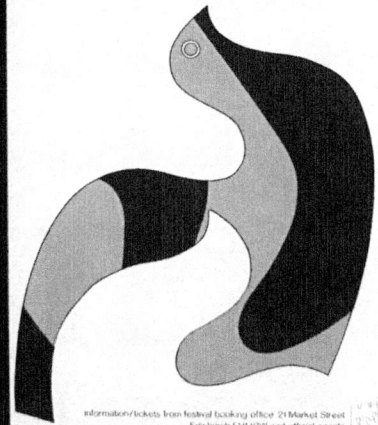

Information/tickets from festival booking office 21 Market Street
Edinburgh EH1 1BW and official agents

The population of Edinburgh almost doubled in size as visitors flocked to the capital for the annual summer Festival this month, which many would argue is the best time to visit Edinburgh as the city becomes the centre of the entertainment world. Visitors and locals alike are treated to performances in the arts, music, theatre, dance, comedy, and literature.

The Fringe started life when eight theatre companies turned up uninvited to the inaugural Edinburgh International Festival in 1947. With all the city's major venues in use, these companies took over smaller, alternative venues for their productions. It is an open access performing arts festival, meaning that there is no selection committee, and anyone may participate, with any type of performance. The official Fringe Programme categorises shows into sections for theatre, comedy, dance, theatre, circus, cabaret, children's shows, musicals, opera, music, spoken word, exhibitions, and events. Comedy is the largest section, making up over one-third of the programme, and the one that in modern times has the highest public profile.

The Edinburgh Festival has not only attracted big names like Maria Callas, Richard Burton and Donald Pleasence, but has become the springboard for many careers. Robin Williams first appeared at the Edinburgh Fringe in 1971 in a production of "The Taming of the Shrew" before going on to be a huge name on both sides of the Atlantic. Peter Cook, who became one of the leading figures in the satire boom of the 60's, first appeared here with Dudley Moore, Alan Bennet and Jonathan Miller in 'Beyond The Fringe'. The Cambridge Footlights Revue appear regularly and have introduced us to actors who have gone on to star in television and cinema such as John Cleese, and Emma Thompson.

FRINGE FESTIVAL - HARDER

```
E S R O T I S I V E S Z L G W B S G X W
V K V S B E Y W U Q T V K X A P E Q J K
I S K T S N D L F P F A S V R C Q C K B
T N B H I O E O A V O R P I K W F L F T
A O H G G I M S I N O P N I H M P Y D F
N I S I C S O L N T O G U V C L N E B R
R T N L U I C X C C B I C L K I K S S I
E C Q T X V M A C O T U T N A C T Q C N
T U T O K E K H A M N P L A O T Y R B G
L D P O K L T R O P E L V L N Q I O A E
A O M F Y E D E E A M Y F H I R U O V P
A R U B Q T O G W N N F R I N G E D N B
A P B O P R W T V I I E R T A E H T Y Q
L I T E R A T U R E A L A R U G U A N I
D N I B O R Z I Q S T H N W E E S K D I
L S E C N A M R O F R E P P U Z J H O Z
U H G R U B N I D E E X Z P U L T T U S
F L A V I T S E F Z T F V Q W C D M U N
E E T T I M M O C G N B Q R J K Z A S Z
L H O W U Q G V L H E U H I S E U N E V
```

POPULATION	EDINBURGH	FLOCKED	FESTIVAL
ENTERTAINMENT	PERFORMANCES	VISITORS	COMEDY
LITERATURE	COMPANIES	THEATRE	FRINGE
INAUGURAL	INTERNATIONAL	ALTERNATIVE	VENUES
PRODUCTIONS	COMMITTEE	PARTICIPATE	ROBIN
FOOTLIGHTS	SPRINGBOARD	TELEVISION	ACTORS

SEPTEMBER 1975

IN THE NEWS

WEEK 1   **"Restaurant Chain in Liquidation"** 'London Eating Houses', a restaurant chain and one of the largest Wimpy bar franchisees, has stopped trading with 800 employees being made redundant.

"London Hilton Bombed" a bomb explosion at the Hilton Hotel, in the West End left two dead and 62 injured. A warning had been telephoned to a newspaper office.

WEEK 2   **"Needles for Nation"** The National Trust has bought the Needles headland, on the Isle of Wight, but the old MOD installations will need to be demolished to allow public access.

"Soviet Shadows" Russian ships shadowed the US Navy's nuclear task group arriving at Portsmouth. *"Right now, off the English Channel, the fishing fleet is not British, but Soviet. I do not think the public realise what has happened,'* the US Commander said.

WEEK 3   **"Housewives in Need"** According to the National Consumer Congress, many husbands hold onto their pay rises, while others pass on less than half for housekeeping. With rising prices, barely 20% of housewives manage.

"Pattie Hearst Arrested" The newspaper heiress, hunted by the FBI for 19 months, was arrested in San Francisco, ending the saga which began in 1974 with her kidnapping by the Symbionese Liberation Army.

WEEK 4   **"Crash Helmet Protest"** 500 Sikhs protested in Slough about a colleague's jail sentence for refusing to pay a £50 fine for twice riding his motorcycle wearing his turban instead of a crash helmet.

"Spaghetti House Siege" Gunmen representing the 'Black Liberation Front' held seven Italians hostage in a Knightsbridge restaurant after releasing one.

HERE IN BRITAIN

"Buy British"

The British motor industry has been criticised for buying car components from foreign manufacturers. There were no British locks, door handles or boot latches on any of the firm's British Leyland 18-22 models, all were being supplied by foreign firms.

In the engine, the Joseph Lucas name is on most of the electrical equipment, but at least 50% of the parts are produced in Japan or Hong Kong, using the Lucas name. 'If we want a British car, it should be a British car and not a British built car with foreign parts'.

AROUND THE WORLD

"Rembrandt Painting Slashed"

Rembrandt's painting 'The Night Watch' was slashed by a man with a bread knife who fought off a museum guard and claimed he 'did it for the Lord.' The attacker arrived shortly after the Rijksmuseum's afternoon opening, heading straight to the painting and slashing it.

The assault made over a dozen cuts, severely damaging a seven-foot section. The restoration is expected to take at least four months. This was the second knife attack on the painting in recent years.

```
Y V X I U U T M D E B M O B H
D U N X Z K G L Z B J K S R T
K Z O M H S E L D E E N R E E
H S I Z O C S T F A H Z I S I
K J T M U O H D Z S S W T T V
P X A E S P E N E H I F T A O
R J D F E G A A Z A T I E U S
O K I N W V R R A D I R H R S
T O U O I M S B V O R Y G A E
E A Q D V A T M I W B J A N W
S M I N E R P E R S L L P T Y
T J L O S Q B R H N J E S F V
L W L L T E M L E H H K I L T
D K A R R E S T E D S X D L Z
M G N I T N I A P Q S F N L T
```

RESTAURANT	LIQUIDATION	LONDON	BOMBED
NEEDLES	SOVIET	SHADOWS	HEARST
ARRESTED	HOUSEWIVES	HELMET	PROTEST
SPAGHETTI	BRITISH	REMBRANDT	PAINTING

MICHAELMAS DAY

Nottingham Goose Fair (main). A goose market (inset).

The Feast of Michael and All Angels Day, known as Michaelmas, was celebrated on the 29th September with religious ceremonies up and down the country. The day traditionally marks the beginning of Autumn and the official shortening of days, marking one of the four 'quarter days' in England. *Lady Day* in March, *Midsummer* in June, *Michaelmas* in September and *Christmas* in December make up the four 'quarter days' in traditional British folklore; spaced three months apart, the days all typically hold religious meaning and fall near an equinox or a solstice. It was on these days that servants were hired or fired, rent was collected and leases were signed. Michaelmas was originally particularly important, as it marked the end of the harvest season, but this became less so following the split from the Catholic Church under Henry VIII in the early 1530s, when the *Harvest Festival* was celebrated a few weeks later on October 10th.

Thousands of families across Britain feasted on a well fattened goose to, according to tradition, protect against financial need in the family for the next year: *'Eat a goose on Michaelmas Day, want not for money all the year.'* Because of this, Michaelmas has earned the nickname *'Goose Day'* and the famous Nottingham Goose fair is still held on the weekend closest to the festival. It stems from a rumour that goose was the food being eaten by Queen Elizabeth I upon hearing of the defeat of the Spanish Armada in 1588, vowing to finish the bird on Michaelmas in celebration.

In British folklore, Michaelmas is the last time that blackberries should be picked, as it was on this day that Lucifer was expelled from heaven, landing on a prickly blackberry bush, and proceeding to scorch it with fiery breath.

MICHAELMAS - HARDER

```
Z W E W X B V L A F L J T E X O N O T N
F E G W A A U L H A E M D Q N P I A O R
P X V P C C E S V F U G Y N I R A L P T
I F R U I A I I N O S A E S C E G L K S
T N G F H T T W C J A E I D K L B A D E
R T E C I S O L S T I C E R N I T N E P
A R I R E B U W Y S U B E W A G O G N T
D M B F H H X H I P A M B B M I D E E E
I O R E T R A U Q P M M I A E O U L T M
T K E V B J C Y C U S A L X Q U J S T B
I K D J X G V T S S P D Z E L S P B A E
O W K O V T N D S F G A N N A E D O F R
N H D G I O I I J E A R X A Q H E U A O
A Q G P R M X M N S V M O U S R C U S G
L C E L E B R A T E D R I M O U L I K T
L H C V Y P P M O S T N A L N M O Y M L
Y Y N Y C A E I W T O R K H I W B H Z D
H G O O S E T C I X V L O K X E P R T W
V O N A I W D E P Z O M P H G O S T A G
K N T A U T U M N F J D U P S Z S E Y U
```

MICHAEL	**ALL ANGELS**	**MICHAELMAS**	**RELIGIOUS**
CELEBRATED	**TRADITIONALLY**	**AUTUMN**	**QUARTER**
SHORTENING	**MIDSUMMER**	**SEPTEMBER**	**BRITISH**
FOLKLORE	**SOLSTICE**	**EQUINOX**	**HARVEST**
SEASON	**FESTIVAL**	**THOUSANDS**	**FAMILIES**
FATTENED	**GOOSE**	**NICKNAME**	**LUCIFER**

OCTOBER 1975

IN THE NEWS

WEEK 1   **"Strict Labelling for Yogurt"** The Food Standards Committee wants stricter rules for labelling yoghurt. It shouldn't be called un-flavoured yoghurt just to distinguish it from yoghurt with added fruit.

"Mine Sweeping Hovercraft" A Royal Navy bomb disposal team used a hovercraft to search for and find a number of unexploded WWII bombs on the Essex marshes.

WEEK 2   **"Beefalo Bull"** The first British supplies of meat from a cow/American bison cross, called a 'beefalo', with leaner cuts and a quarter the price of beef will soon be on sale.

"Not So Sweet Tooth" Manufacturers report that Britain's sweet consumption has fallen by a tenth since last year, but that hasn't prevented the cost of sweets sold from rising by more than 25%.

WEEK 3   **"Sold Out"** Tickets for the first Concorde flights went on sale with the first three journeys fully booked. People on a register kept over the past 11 years had first choice.

"Roof Garden to Stay" The Biba store in Kensington High Street has closed after only two years of trading. However, a preservation order has been placed on the roof garden.

WEEK 4   **"Slow Down for Chrysler"** Chrysler's car assembly plant is to work only eight days in November and three days in December. The company has only worked three and four-day weeks since September.

"Rock Star Turned Sculptor" Tommy Steele has given a statue called 'Bermondsey Boy', based on and sculpted by himself, to the new Rotherhithe Civic Centre.

HERE IN BRITAIN

"Conker Championships"

64 contenders entered the 11th World Conker Championships at Ashton, in Northamptonshire. Players from around the world took part in the tournament, both teams and individuals competed in a knock-out format, with titles for men's, women's and youth categories.

The event began in 1965 when a group of anglers held a conker contest at the local pub when the weather was too bad to go fishing. A small collection was made for charity, since then the event has raised at least £2,500 for visually impaired people every year.

AROUND THE WORLD

"He is The Greatest"

Muhammad Ali retained his world heavyweight boxing title when Joe Frazier's corner stopped the fight in the 14th round in their third and final fight. The 'Thrilla in Manila' as the event was dubbed, was televised from the Philippines and streamed around the world.

Some sources estimate that the fight was watched by around 1billion people worldwide. This included 100 million viewers on closed-circuit television and 500,000 pay-per-view buys on HBO. Ali won by technical knockout (TKO) and then collapsed with exhaustion after being pronounced the winner.

October 1975 - Easier

```
F M A R C H E S S G U X E E J
R Y N R E L S Y R H C I P L L
O O G C X X E D R O C N O C X
T G N H S T R I C T X O J A K
P U I A J K T J T F J O T Y B
L R L M C N H D O A A F D K D
U T L P B E T N O R C K N Y A
C X E I U D M P T C O G R L M
S F B O F R H U H R N N Z B M
N K A N M A Q X I E K I N M A
O J L S M G H K L V E P X E H
S G T H E F F P M O R E Z S U
I P I I J O J O C H S E N S M
B Z B P O O E D E E R W P A P
S L U S Q R G S Z W K S G J M
```

STRICT	LABELLING	YOGURT	SWEEPING
HOVERCRAFT	MARCHES	BISON	TOOTH
CONCORDE	ROOF GARDEN	CHRYSLER	ASSEMBLY
SCULPTOR	CHAMPIONSHIPS	MUHAMMAD	CONKER

TRAFALGAR DAY

Trafalgar Day was marked in Britain this year with the traditional naval ceremony of colours aboard HMS Victory in Portsmouth. The white ensign and Union Jack were raised on the 150-year-old wooden galleon, before a flag sequence read Admiral Horatio Nelson's famous message to his fleet: *'England expects that every man will do his duty ...'*. Later, all over Britain the traditional Trafalgar Day Dinner was held, a grand affair with long-standing traditions including parading the baron of beef, Ship of the Line chocolate replica of the HMS Victory, reading of the historical dispatches, toasts and more.

Trafalgar Day is the annual celebration observed on October 21, commemorating the victory of the Royal Navy over the French and Spanish forces at the Battle of Trafalgar in 1805. The battle came at the height of the Napoleonic Wars, where France was the dominant European military power and were rapidly expanding under the leadership of Napoleon. Nevertheless, the Royal Navy proved that, under the command of Admiral Nelson, Britain still ruled the seas. On the Franco-Spanish front were 33-line ships, five frigates and two brigs, while the Royal Navy had just 27-line ships, four frigates, one schooner and one cutter. Despite being outnumbered, outflanked and hundreds of miles from the English Channel, Nelson employed ambitious tactics, capturing 18 French ships, and forcing Admiral Villeneuve to surrender. The British fleet he commanded consisted of warships built of wood, driven by sails, and equipped on both sides with cannons. After leading his fleet to one of the greatest maritime victories in history, Admiral Nelson died aboard HMS Victory after being hit by a Spanish musket ball. Nelson was fanned and brought lemonade and watered wine to drink and stayed alive until his deck commander confirmed the full surrender of French forces, three hours later.

TRAFALGAR DAY - HARDER

```
Q J I B R I T A I N H N S C P D Y Z U X
A O C H O C O L A T E G S L N J F E U Y
A E B I E W D X U B E C N E U Q E S T H
N W B J K K O O A T D O M I N A N T O R
O S K G T L M U P E Y Z W Q N C E R A Q
E V Z Y N S A U Y P E W N G E X A G D N
L G Y J T A H M O R L V I W P T L J E O
L K N R V U E I M A O S P S I A O L A Q
A B O I G H M P C Y N T F O F W S I Y X
G P M W T C S I O E R Z C A W O J L X G
Q W E H T A R N R R H O R I N E A Q K Y
N Y R I V O R N O J U T T S V N W T H U
C T E E T R A O C N Q E W C O S K D K I
F D C S K V U C M C N Z R I I A M D C K
N O I T A R B E L E C A T P C V N H F A
O H R L L H B X Q D M I C I W A I O I G
L A R I M D A U D X D M L N S Y H H O R
V K W V B T T B N A E P O S E Q E Y J K
C X E C N A R F R C E F E C O U Q E A E
P O J Y N Y E T S R C I N O E L O P A N
```

TRAFALGAR   BRITAIN   TRADITIONAL   NAVAL
CEREMONY   HMS VICTORY   PORTSMOUTH   ENSIGN
GALLEON   SEQUENCE   ADMIRAL   NELSONS
HORATIO   CHOCOLATE   REPLICA   VICTORY
HISTORICAL   CELEBRATION   COMMEMORATING   FRANCE
NAPOLEONIC   DOMINANT   EUROPEAN   CANNONS

IN THE NEWS

WEEK 1   **"North Sea Oil on Stream"** The Queen pressed a button in Dyce, Aberdeen, to inaugurate the flow of North Sea oil from BP's Forties field, the largest oilfield so far discovered in the British sector and is now pumping £28 a second into the economy.

    "Blast Furnace Explosion" An explosion in a 190-ton ladle of molten iron killed five and injured 14 blasting apart the 40' roof at the British Steel's complex at Scunthorpe.

WEEK 2   **"Turkey's Off"** Due to the cost, 72,000 Buckinghamshire children who stay for school lunches, will have an ordinary meal instead of the traditional Christmas fare this year.

    "Speed Limits Stay" The temporary 50 mph and 60 mph speed limits on many roads, imposed last December as a fuel-saving measure, will stay in place for another year.

WEEK 3   **"Police Board Pop Music Ship"** Radio Caroline, went off the air after Essex police boarded its headquarters ship the 'Mia Amigo', in the Thames Estuary. Four men will appear in court at Southend.

    "Reckless Driver" Les McKeown, the 20-year-old lead singer of the Bay City Rollers, appeared at Edinburgh Sheriff Court charged with killing an elderly woman while driving 'recklessly' in the city. *"I didn't realise I'd hit her as I didn't feel any impact,"* he said.

WEEK 4   **"Hands Up!"** Christmas supermarket shoppers were advised by an MP to hold goods they have picked up from counters, over their heads, to avoid wrongful prosecution during the 'Christmas shoplifting season'.

    "You Can't Beat the Budget" The Home Office has authorised 4,000 letters to be sent out, warning that 'overlapping' colour television licences taken out to beat the April Budget increases, will be revoked.

HERE IN BRITAIN

"Women Lose Out"

The first unintended consequences of the Sex Discrimination Act emerged yesterday, as women in Liverpool lost access to cheaper train fares for shopping trips to London. British Rail had offered special 'women's day tickets', aimed at encouraging housewives to travel, with notable success.

However, British Rail lawyers have determined these offers along with phasing out women's-only waiting rooms at stations, must end to comply with the new Act, which aims to prevent gender discrimination.

AROUND THE WORLD

"Complaining Housewives"

A debate occurred between the Polish party leader, aided by the Prime Minister and several hundred Communist Party women, who complained about the hardships faced by housewives in Poland. The televised discussion focused on the shortage and poor quality of consumer goods.

Both officials acknowledged the country's economic and housing challenges, admitting many products were substandard suggesting it would be 'ideal if each worker desired to buy the products they produced.'

NOVEMBER 1975 - EASIER

```
M J P S L I M I T S Z A J N O
Q W O M H H A R D S H I P S Y
K O L N G N I N I A L P M O C
N N I V D N D E R I S E D B D
O O S X N E Q O G N E E U Q
I D H B E L J M B E S Q H O R
S N J B M H Z D O M A E R T S
O O I X O W X V A I O F Q R T
L L F M W Z T J Y Z V D P W L
P E C A N R U F K D R I V E R
X N I G U S H E C I L O P M C
E A S S E L K C E R R P E O O
Q T I C S E V I W E S U O H E
U O B T E G D U B S R C K S C
J M K B K A Y E Z Q X H L W H
```

STREAM	QUEEN	FURNACE	EXPLOSION
LIMITS	POLICE	RECKLESS	DRIVER
BUDGET	WOMEN	LONDON	COMPLAINING
HOUSEWIVES	POLISH	HARDSHIPS	DESIRED

STIR UP SUNDAY

'Stir-up Sunday' is a centuries old tradition, where on the last Sunday before Advent, housewives start 'stirring up' their Christmas puddings. It is a family affair, and even children are allowed to help weigh out and mix all the ingredients ready for steaming the pudding. Everyone is expected to take a turn to stir the pudding mix, for each person can make a special wish for the year ahead. Traditionally, the pudding should be stirred from east to west, in honour of the Wise Men who travelled from the East to visit the baby Jesus.

Rich Christmas puddings and fruit cakes benefit from being made this much in advance because it allows the flavours to intensify, and the colour deepen over time. Puddings can be re-steamed each week and many people will also 'feed' their cakes by pricking the base and pouring an eggcup full of brandy or rum over it, before wrapping it up again carefully to preserve the moisture. By Christmas, a good cake or pudding will be 'black and rotten' – very rich indeed!

The Christmas pudding originated in the 14th-century as a sort of porridge, originally known as 'frumenty', which bore little resemblance to the pudding we know today but, in the 17th century, changes to the recipe were made. It was thickened with eggs, breadcrumbs, dried fruit and beer or spirits were added – and it came to resemble something a bit more like a sweet pudding. Nowadays, the ingredients include raisins, currants, suet, brown sugar, breadcrumbs, carrot, mixed peel, flour, mixed spices, eggs, milk and brandy, which are all essential for keeping qualities. Puddings were traditionally boiled in a 'pudding cloth', although today are usually steamed in a basin, then brought to the table with a sprig of holly, doused in brandy and set alight.

STIR UP SUNDAY - HARDER

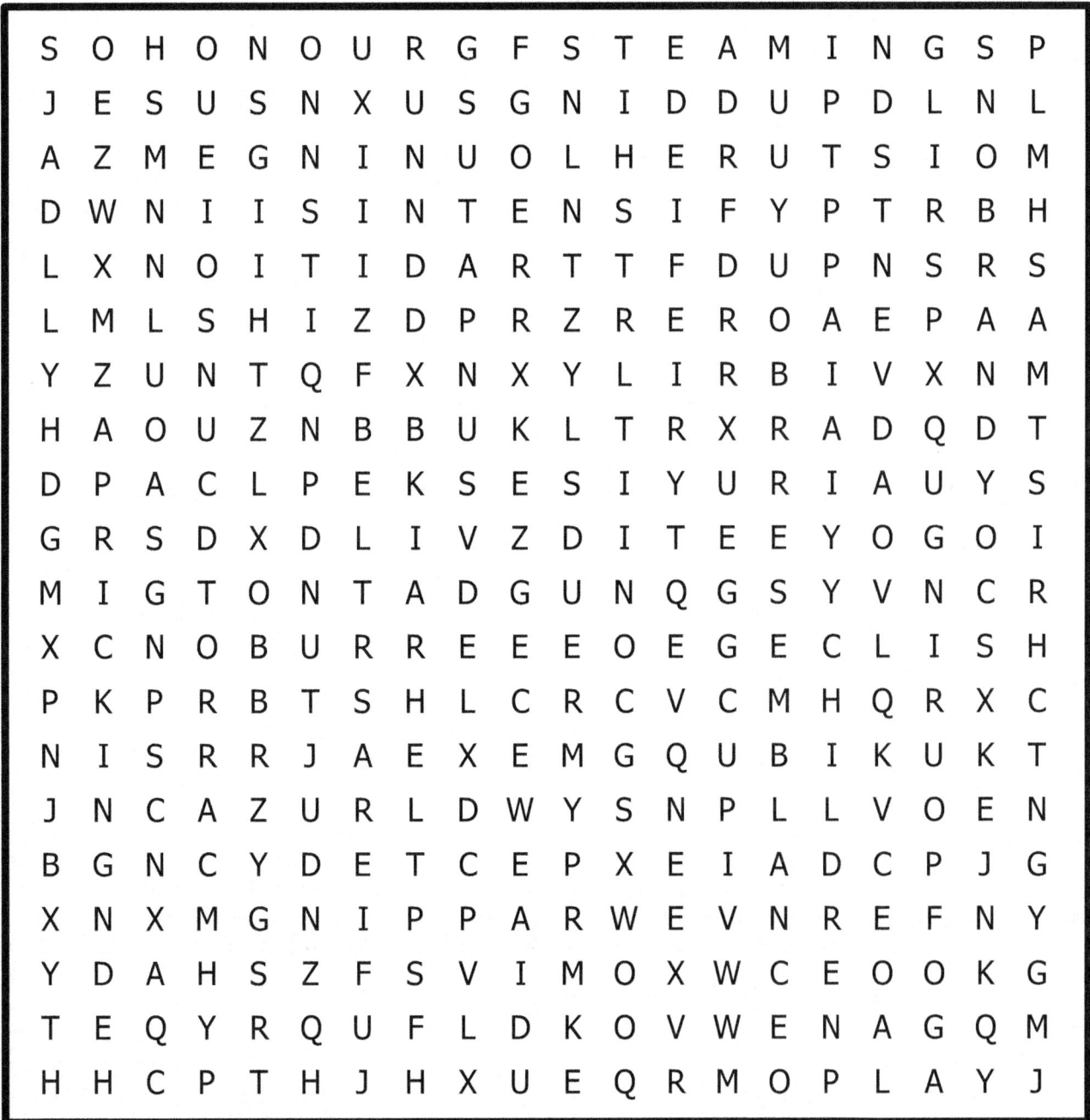

```
S O H O N O U R G F S T E A M I N G S P
J E S U S N X U S G N I D D U P D L N L
A Z M E G N I N U O L H E R U T S I O M
D W N I I S I N T E N S I F Y P T R B H
L X N O I T I D A R T T F D U P N S R S
L M L S H I Z D P R Z R E R O A E P A A
Y Z U N T Q F X N X Y L I R B I V X N M
H A O U Z N B B U K L T R X R A D Q D T
D P A C L P E K S E S I Y U R I A U Y S
G R S D X D L I V Z D I T E E Y O G O I
M I G T O N T A D G U N Q G S Y V N C R
X C N O B U R R E E E O E G E C L I S H
P K P R B T S H L C R C V C M H Q R X C
N I S R R J A E X E M G Q U B I K U K T
J N C A Z U R L D W Y S N P L L V O E N
B G N C Y D E T C E P X E I A D C P J G
X N X M G N I P P A R W E V N R E F N Y
Y D A H S Z F S V I M O X W C E O O K G
T E Q Y R Q U F L D K O V W E N A G Q M
H H C P T H J H X U E Q R M O P L A Y J
```

STIR-UP	CENTURIES	TRADITION	ADVENT
CHRISTMAS	PUDDINGS	EXPECTED	CHILDREN
INGREDIENTS	STEAMING	HONOUR	JESUS
TRAVELLED	INTENSIFY	PRICKING	POURING
EGGCUP	BRANDY	WRAPPING	MOISTURE
PORRIDGE	RESEMBLANCE	DOUSED	CARROT

DECEMBER 1975

IN THE NEWS

WEEK 1   **"Kirby Disaster Area"** Merseyside police have called for investment in Kirkby, blaming government neglect and inadequate infrastructure for economic decline and crime there, despite good local support.

"107 Schools Go Independent" At least 107 of the 173 direct-grant grammar schools in England and Wales have decided to become independent rather than comprehensive.

WEEK 2   **"Christmas Cheese Ceremony"** The Christmas Cheese ceremony of 1692, took place at the Royal Hospital, in Chelsea, where a large wheel of cheese was blessed, before being cut with a sword, by one of the pensioners.

"Fog Affects Flights and Roads" Ice and dense fog seriously disrupted both road and air journeys, with visibility as low as one yard in Kent.

WEEK 3   **"First Female QC"** Judge Patricia Coles has become the first woman of Lincoln's Inn to be made a QC after being sworn in as circuit judge by the Lord Chancellor.

"Smelly Dispute" 21 workers at the Liverpool Leyland Triumph car plant went on strike complaining about the smell from stray cats. 600 men stopped work while cleaners spent 45 minutes scrubbing the floor, whereupon the men protested that the floor was too wet and dangerous to work on.

WEEK 4   **"All at Sea"** Light-keeper Donald McLeod said goodbye to his family in Stromness, Orkney, to spend a month on Sule Skerry, 30 miles west of Orkney in the Atlantic, Britain's most distant lighthouse.

"Salvation Army" Up to 2,200 of London's down-and-outs enjoyed some Christmas cheer at Salvation Army hostels with free meals, including turkey with all the trimmings.

HERE IN BRITAIN

"Laddo The Lion"

Laddo's owner is ready to defy a West Midland's court ruling forbidding him to keep a lion at his home in Cradley Heath. He appeared in court with a lion tamer, who lives at the same address. They were charged with behaving in a manner likely to cause a breach of the peace, by taking a wild animal for a tour around Birmingham.

The case was adjourned for nine days. The accused commented, *"I am taking my lion out and I do not care if I get arrested and put in jail. He needs exercise badly."*

AROUND THE WORLD

"Fiji Island Paradise"

The American Theatre Film Corporation of Los Angeles wanted to film a thrilling event similar to that described in Peter Benchley's novel 'Jaws' and they chose the tropical island of Fiji for the location. The event was to be a fight to the death between an experienced Australian diver and a 17' killer shark.

However, the fight, which would have netted the diver a fee of $1m, has been banned by the Fiji Government, as they objected to their island paradise being made the site for a blood sport.

DECEMBER 1975 - EASIER

```
S T N E M N R E V O G W W P H
U L I S M E L L Y N B V F H N
J A U S T R A L I A N Z O F O
B X H U A I J O Z M S D Z O I
S T H G I L F E B E C G T R L
J I K X Y S L X N R H S U B I
O L Q F X G Y X E I O A K I Z
A D I S A S T E R C O L D D I
E S E E H C W J P A L V V D S
Y G E Z U X C F M N S A F I L
L P R C J F E M A L E T X N A
K W C H R I S T M A S I K G N
C B B G D H I C B L O O D Q D
I D D B S B O N Q Y D N Z I W
R H A B T W E S I D A R A P T
```

DISASTER	GOVERNMENT	SCHOOLS	CHRISTMAS
CHEESE	FLIGHTS	FEMALE	SMELLY
SALVATION	FORBIDDING	AMERICAN	LION
ISLAND	PARADISE	AUSTRALIAN	BLOOD

Norway's annual gift of a Christmas tree is in pride of place at Trafalgar Square, although the original excitement over the tree and its lights has somewhat dimmed over the years. The Acton Gazette led with the spartan headline, *'The traditional lighting-up of the Trafalgar Square Christmas tree is taking place tomorrow,'* and one gentleman due to retire commented, *'Tree? Who cares?'*

The first tree was sent from Oslo in 1947 as a token of gratitude to the British people for their help during the second world war when Great Britain was Norway's closest ally. London was where the Norwegian King Haakon VII and his government fled as their country was occupied, and it was from here that much of Norway's resistance movement was organised. Both the BBC and its Norwegian counterpart NRK would broadcast in Norwegian from London, something that was both an important source of information and a boost of morale for those who remained in Norway, where people would listen in secret to their forbidden radios. The idea to send a pine to Britain was first conceived by the Norwegian naval commando, Mons Urangsvå, who sent a tree from the island of Hisøy which had been cut down during a raid to London in 1942 as a gift to King Haakon and King George V decided that it should be installed in Trafalgar Square where it stood *'evergreen with defiant hope'*.

The trees come from the snow-covered forest area surrounding Oslo, known as "Oslomarka", an area populated with moose, lynx, roe deer, and even the odd wolf, and legions of pine trees. A worthy tree is located by the head forester and space is cleared around it to allow light from all angles, and it is tended through the years to secure optimal growth.

TRAFALGAR TREE - HARDER

```
U J X L I G H T S I K C E L T I V F T R
F L N M C N P U A D S O I D A R Y A D G
L O T O G H A X Q A P I U Y W X A K B P
P N J R N P O I V V I Y G J D G A U C D
Q D E K I P C K G V D A S E C O N D D H
P O N R D V C L K E Q Z X M G H F E O U
Q N M P N G U A Q E W J H R E A F S C G
T G C F U L P M Q U V R A W D I L W O C
Y N O O O U I I Q I H T O B A O D B M H
K X U R R O E T A G I S R N K L I K M R
E U N B R X D P N T A O T O Y N U N A I
V A T I U P O O U E A Z S P A R T A N S
E N R D S G X D M D M C E Q D I E W D T
R N Y D W M E Q C O L E T T E Z N F O M
G U K E J G C A E W K A T V T R Y I B A
R A Q N Z K S X A X L T C I F E A P F S
E L R J Y T V F C P K E V I C O J U P U
E V U R A G L A F A R T G V E X E A Q A
N L M B T G E N T L E M A N G D E B K S
S C J N T O R P Y F W R I J B W B D O O
```

NORWEGIAN	ANNUAL	CHRISTMAS	LIGHTS
TRAFALGAR	EXCITEMENT	SQUARE	GAZETTE
SPARTAN	GENTLEMAN	GRATITUDE	SECOND
LONDON	COUNTRY	BROADCAST	OCCUPIED
COMMANDO	FORBIDDEN	RADIOS	DEFIANT
EVERGREEN	OSLO	SURROUNDING	OPTIMAL

1970 - 1974

1970:

Jan: The age of majority for most legal purposes was reduced from 21 to 18 under terms of the Family Law Reform Act 1969.

Mar: Ian Smith declares Rhodesia a Republic and the British government refuses to recognise the new state.

1971:

Feb: Decimal Day. The UK and the Republic of Ireland both change to decimal currency.

Mar: The 'Daily Sketch', Britain's oldest tabloid newspaper is absorbed by the 'Daily Mail' after 62 years.

1972:

June: The 'Watergate' scandal begins in Richard Nixon's administration in the US.

Sep: The school leaving age in the UK was raised from 15 to 16 for pupils leaving at the end of the academic year.

1973:

Jan: The United Kingdom joins the European Economic Community, later to become the EU.

Sep: The IRA detonate bombs in Manchester and Victoria Station London and two days later, Oxford St. and Sloane Square.

1974:

Jan: Until March, the 3-day week is introduced by the Conservative Government to conserve electricity during the miners' strike.

Nov: 21 people are killed and 182 injured when the IRA set bombs in two Birmingham pubs.

1974: McDonald's open their first UK restaurant in South London. The traditional café was losing out, slow ordering and service with food served at tables was not as appealing as the clean, fast service and lower prices of this new fast food.

1974: In February, Harold Wilson becomes Prime Minister for the second time (first 1964-70) with a minority Government after Edward Heath resigns having failed to clinch a coalition with the Liberals. In the second general election of the year in October, Labour win with a majority of only 3 seats.

```
T  Y  B  G  S  Z  F  H  H  J  P  F  M  P  N
E  T  A  G  R  E  T  A  W  D  I  K  K  V  M
L  Z  U  C  W  C  O  M  M  U  N  I  T  Y  R
C  I  Y  L  I  A  D  H  D  U  O  E  J  P  R
B  C  R  H  O  D  E  S  I  A  N  C  T  I  E
F  I  N  S  D  L  A  N  O  D  C  M  D  G  T
H  L  N  I  S  B  M  O  B  U  A  B  L  Y  S
C  B  E  G  A  G  N  I  V  A  E  L  M  W  E
T  U  L  R  E  S  T  A  U  R  A  N  T  F  H
E  P  E  C  O  N  O  M  I  C  I  K  C  D  C
K  E  N  G  A  P  T  J  X  K  J  A  M  J  N
S  R  Y  N  B  F  O  G  H  T  A  E  H  O  A
E  K  L  Y  V  X  V  R  Z  T  A  J  I  G  M
N  O  S  L  I  W  M  N  A  E  P  O  R  U  E
Y  A  D  L  A  M  I  C  E  D  B  A  Z  S  Z
```

RHODESIA	REPUBLIC	DECIMAL DAY	DAILY
SKETCH	WATERGATE	LEAVING AGE	EUROPEAN
ECONOMIC	COMMUNITY	BOMBS IN	MANCHESTER
MCDONALDS	RESTAURANT	WILSON	HEATH

THE 70s MAJOR NEWS - 2

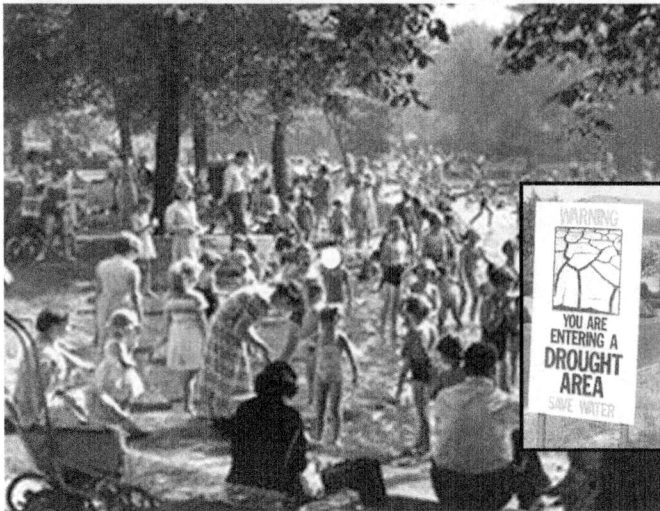

In June and July 1976, the UK experienced a heat wave. Temperatures peak at 35.9° and the whole country suffers a severe drought. Forest fires broke out, crops failed, and reservoirs dried up causing serious water shortages. The heatwave also produced swarms of ladybirds across the south and east.

On the 7th June,1977, more than one million people lined the streets of London to watch the Queen and Prince Phillip lead a procession in the golden state coach, to St Paul's at the start of a week of the Queen's Silver Jubilee celebrations – 25 years on the throne. People all over the country held street or village parties to celebrate, more than 100,000 cards were received by the Queen and 30,000 Jubilee medals were given out.

1975 - 1979

1975:
Feb: Margaret Thatcher defeats Edward Heath to become the first female leader of the Conservative Party.

Apr: The Vietnam War ends with the Fall of Saigon to the Communists. South Vietnam surrenders unconditionally.

1976:
Mar: Harold Wilson announces his resignation as Prime Minister and James Callaghan is elected to the position in April.

Oct: The Intercity 125 high speed passenger train is introduced. Initially Paddington to Bristol and south Wales.

1977:
Jan: Jimmy Carter is sworn in as the 39th President of the United States, succeeding Gerald Ford.

Sep: Freddie Laker launches his 'Skytrain' with a single fare, Gatwick to New York, at £59 compared to £189.

1978:
Aug: Louise Brown becomes the world's first human born 'in vitro fertilisation' – test tube baby.

Nov: An industrial dispute shuts down The Times newspaper – until November 1979.

1979:
Mar: Airey Neave, politician and WW2 veteran, is blown up in the House of Commons car park by the Irish National Liberation Army.

May: Margaret Thatcher becomes the first female Prime Minister of the United Kingdom. The Conservatives win a 43 seat

```
P N D S U D Q B C N C E Z P C A K Q F L
E T E P Z J U F K R C W U U B M E I U T
S V Y H P I U O I W M K N D J F G C R Z
S T R E E T S B W R S E V E R E P T T C
T H A T C H E R I V E Y V I K K E E Y V
V S J P Y Z Z Y Y L N S A R K T M G W Z
I R S Z N E C R B N E A B D R P W F H L
E I S K B L C T A J C E T R E R M Z O R
T O G S U P D N D C W K E R O S B A L E
N V J T A O U U V R Z J A G R K M X E V
A R Y A X E A O Z Y O T C E X T E R L L
M E F T D P I C B K U U F A E K P O Q I
T S H E L N N B R R J F G N R P S J U S
N E J C I O T K E Y U L Z H M T C R X T
E R U O N I E S G S C W C B T W E W S R
D Y G A E L R E H P R Q C M Q O G R K Z
L N N C D L C B X H E A T W A V E B X G
O W O H T I I A Z O L I A F S P O R C K
G N N Z H M T H S D R I B Y D A L G V T
Q W P K E G Y U U P X B T S E R O F O D
```

HEAT WAVE	**TEMPERATURES**	**WHOLE**	**COUNTRY**
SUFFERS	**SEVERE**	**DROUGHT**	**FOREST**
FIRES BROKE OUT	**CROPS FAIL**	**RESERVOIRS**	**DRIED UP**
LADYBIRDS	**MILLION PEOPLE**	**LINED THE**	**STREETS**
GOLDEN	**STATE COACH**	**SILVER**	**JUBILEE**
THATCHER	**VIETNAM**	**INTERCITY**	**CARTER**

THE HOME IN THE 70S - 1

Increasing Comfort and Prosperity

Homes became brighter and more comfortable in the 1970's. Teenagers could lie on the 'impossible to clean', loopy shag pile carpet watching films on VHS video cassettes or watch live programmes on the family's colour television set.

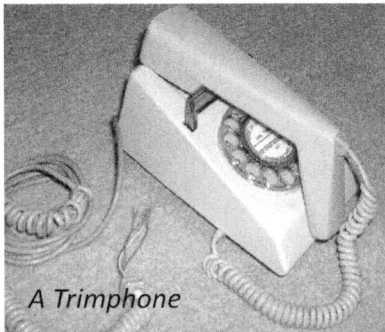

A Trimphone

The ubiquitous macramé owl, or plant holder complete with trailing spider plant, might dangle in the corner adjacent to the bulky, stone faced, rustic fireplace. Bathroom suites were often Avocado green and 'downstairs loos' were a statement of the houseowners ideals! If you were one of the 35% of households in Britain to own a telephone, you could catch up with friends and family on the new 'warbling' Trimphone, maybe sitting on your bright, floral covered couch.

Labour Saving Devices

The previous decade had been prosperous and the advances in technology continued such that by the 1970s, most households had many labour-saving devices. Sales of freezers rose rapidly in the 70s and by 1974, one in ten households had a freezer - mainly full of peas, chips and fish fingers but also ice cream, previously a rare treat, and in large quantities. Bulk buying food meant less time shopping and the Magimix food processor which added a choice of blades and attachments to a standard liquidiser, made home cooking more adventurous.

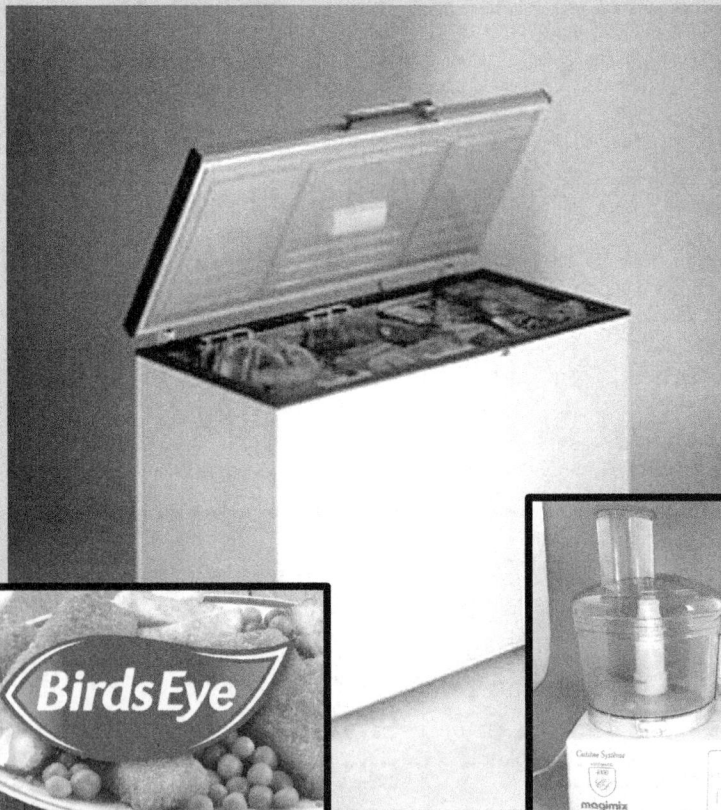

THE 70s HOME - EASIER

```
R Y M A E R C E C I S K E M O
P C U U W X T R I M P H O N E
T M R L V T R U O L O C U M Y
N K Q G N I L B R A W O C F G
A S I U L Q E C A L P E R I F
L G K S S R E G A N E E T S P
P N V P P H C U O C Q V F H R
F I T I D M A G I M I X L F O
G S N D N M F B I T F F O I S
J A O E X O R K S U I B R N P
F E E R N J E O N U J G A G E
M R D V J T E X T Y G L L E R
O C I H I X Z H W B R X L R I
H N V X F G E F M V J Y G S T
O I W N M K R W V K M G O N Y
```

INCREASING	PROSPERITY	TEENAGERS	VIDEO
COLOUR TV	SPIDER	PLANT	FIREPLACE
WARBLING	TRIMPHONE	FLORAL	COUCH
FREEZER	FISH FINGERS	MAGIMIX	ICE CREAM

Teenage Home Entertainment

Teenagers covered their bedroom walls with posters of their favourite bands and actors, ranging from Rod Stewart and the Boomtown Rats to Olivia Newton-John and Robert Redford. The lucky ones listening to top ten singles on their own stereo record deck which had replaced the old Dansette player.

If they wanted to play the new video games, they typically went to an arcade, but in 1975, Atari PONG was released, the first commercially successful video game you could play at home on your television. Based on a simple two-dimensional graphical representation of a tennis-like game, two players used paddles to hit a ball back and forth on a black and white screen. It captivated audiences and its success influenced developers to invent more and increasingly sophisticated games for the home market.

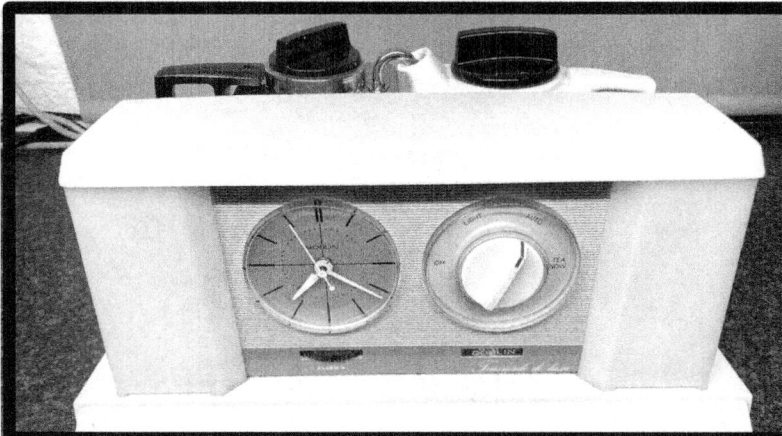

The luxury of a Goblin Teasmade, the automatic tea-maker and alarm clock, revolutionised early morning tea.

THE 70s HOME - HARDER

```
K D B A N D S A N D A C T O R S Z X B I
F S A E T E N E O Z R S E C N E I D U A
Q F K N X I D E M Q N O I S I V E L E T
V K G D S Y Q M W U E Q B N B B D E D G
A C C E J E F U G T M T B E Q V X F M R
I E Y C N C T X Y E O B F R R V S U O M
V D A A I J S T J N E N E P I T A Q T K
I O D L L A G X E H L J D M Z K C F G
L E X P B E S I I E T G E O R C F M M D
O R W E O E G R X R Y O L H H O Q L R V
G E H R G M U R Q T G A U V E N O O O P
A T O L R O Y I O A I M F H O V F M D O
T S M V V M B Q M I G Y S G C D I W S S
A Y E A W T J E D N E U S K E W X T T T
R Q F F Q G S J A M O V E R T N T I E E
I C A P T I V A T E D H C L J R O M W R
P Z B Z O Q I U H N X T C U G D T S A S
O S T C F A U T G T L H U L L F G D R X
N L A N W O T M O O B X S W Y A X V T A
G U W N O H J J J T E E N A G E S J S U S
```

TEENAGE	HOME	ENTERTAINMENT	BEDROOM
POSTERS	FAVOURITE	BANDS AND ACTORS	ROD STEWART
BOOMTOWN	OLIVIA	NEWTON JOHN	ROBERT
REDFORD	STEREO DECK	REPLACED	DANSETTE
VIDEO GAMES	ATARI PONG	COMMERCIALLY	SUCCESSFUL
AT HOME	TELEVISION	CAPTIVATED	AUDIENCES

THE 70S ART AND CULTURE 1

1970 - 1974

1970 Laurence Olivier becomes the first actor to be made a Lord. He is given a life peerage in the Queen's Birthday Honours list.
The first Glastonbury Festival was held, called the Worthy Farm Pop Festival. About 1500 attended.

1971 Coco Chanel, the French fashion designer died. (Born 1883)
The 'Blue Peter' presenters buried a time capsule in the grounds of BBC Television Centre, due to be opened on the first episode in 2000.
Mr Tickle, the first of the Mr Men books is published.

1972 'Jesus Christ Superstar', the Tim Rice & Andrew Lloyd Webber musical opens in the West End.
John Betjeman is appointed Poet Laureate.

1973 The British Library is established by merger of the British Museum Library & the National Lending Library for Science & Technology.
Series 1 of the BBC sitcom, 'Last of the Summer Wine' begins. There are eventually, 31 series.

1974 'Tinker, Tailor, Soldier, Spy' the first of John Le Carré's novel featuring the ageing spymaster, George Smiley, is published.
The Terracotta Army of Qin Shi Huang, thousands of life-size clay models of soldiers, horses and chariots, is discovered at Xi'an in China.

Milton Keynes Shopping Centre

1975 - 1979

1975 Donald Coggan is enthroned as the Archbishop of Canterbury.
Bill Gates and Paul Allen found Microsoft in Albuquerque, New Mexico.

1976 Trevor Nunn's memorable production of 'Macbeth' opens at Stratford-upon-Avon, with Ian McKellan and Judi Dench in the lead roles.
The Royal National Theatre on the South Bank opens.
Agatha Christie's last novel, Sleeping Murder, a Miss Marple story is published posthumously.

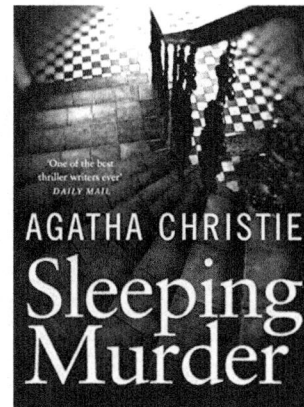

1977 Luciano Pavarotti makes his television debut singing in Puccini's La Boheme in the television debut of 'Live from the Met'.
Mike Leigh's satire on the aspirations and tastes of the new middle class emerging in the 70's, 'Abigail's Party', opened at the Hampstead Theatre starring Alison Steadman.

1978 The Andrew Lloyd Webber musical 'Evita' opens in London.
The arcade video game, 'Space Invaders' is released.

1979 Margaret Thatcher opens the new Central Milton Keynes Shopping Centre, the largest indoor shopping centre in Britain.
Anthony Blunt, British art historian and former Surveyor of the Queen's Pictures, in exposed as a double agent for the Soviets during WW2.
The Sony Walkman, portable cassette player is released.

```
I  W  U  F  E  S  T  I  V  A  L  J  E  H  W
A  T  P  B  J  R  A  M  N  P  L  J  I  Q  N
O  L  J  S  N  D  H  I  A  B  S  B  T  K  P
Z  A  D  E  L  T  I  C  M  J  R  A  S  N  A
I  U  R  C  I  V  E  R  K  H  E  A  I  B  T
T  R  E  A  B  M  F  O  L  R  D  G  R  R  T
T  E  I  P  R  A  G  S  A  O  A  A  H  I  O
O  N  V  S  A  N  G  O  W  T  V  T  C  T  C
R  C  I  M  R  S  R  F  K  B  N  H  E  I  A
A  E  L  C  Y  M  I  T  K  Z  I  A  F  S  R
V  I  O  U  X  Q  F  L  X  N  G  G  N  H  R
A  J  E  V  I  T  A  G  K  Q  G  R  W  D  E
P  Y  R  U  B  N  O  T  S  A  L  G  P  W  T
J  F  S  B  L  U  E  P  E  T  E  R  R  X  L
C  K  N  W  C  C  U  B  H  J  S  U  I  P  S
```

LAWRENCE	OLIVIER	GLASTONBURY	FESTIVAL
BLUE PETER	BRITISH	LIBRARY	TERRACOTTA
MICROSOFT	AGATHA	CHRISTIE	PAVAROTTI
EVITA	SPACE	INVADERS	WALKMAN

Pavarotti at the Met.

It was in his third season at the Metropolitan Opera House in New York that Luciano Pavarotti, the operatic tenor, would skyrocket to stardom. The company imported Covent Garden's production of Donizetti's *La Fille du Régiment* in 1972 as a vehicle for Joan Sutherland. The great Australian diva enjoyed a huge triumph, but the surprise for the audience was the young Italian tenor by her side who shared an equal part in the phenomenal success. This was the historic first Met performance telecast live on PBS as part of the long-running series that continues to the present day.

The Terracotta Army

'The Qin Tomb Terracotta Warriors and Horses' was constructed between 246-206BC as an afterlife guard for China's First Emperor, Qin Shihuang, from whom, China gets its name. He ordered it built to remember the army he led to triumph over other warring states, and to unite China.

The tomb and the army were all made by hand by some 700,000 artisans and labourers, and comprises thousands of life-size soldiers, each with different facial features and expressions, clothing, hairstyles and gestures, arranged in battle array.

All figures face east, towards the ancient enemies of Qin State, in rectangular formations and three separate vaults include rows of kneeling and standing archers, chariot war configurations and mixed forces of infantry, horse drawn chariots plus numerous soldiers armed with long spears, daggers and halberds.

ART AND CULTURE - HARDER

```
C I Y C O C Y W H P Z K S R V R L N Q M
D A L Z G V P Y M R A F B Z M I T U T E
B D F I R S T E M P E R O R F V K V K T
X Q P D A H W E G I G K V E S Q M T R R
S S B M L P U T R V F Q S O J Z N Y M O
R S P O B D P E L U C I N A S Y M T V P
E R T D I E C K D T Z O H K B R I B K O
H O S R P T D C A E H K O C K N E E S L
C I Q A E E Z O L L E S Y I C A M Q T I
R R B T T R S R L E S Z E S R I S P O T
A R F S S R T Y M C U U Z D R L W U I A
P A J O A A N K A A O F H N O A S W R N
U W R T E C E S D S H P Y A N R S B A U
X I Y X E O V A E T A U E S A T E Y H T
W J Q N C T O A G L R L F U I S C H C Q
R R G Q A T C A W I E O M O C U C A P I
N C H I F A R L L V P J P H U A U N E V
Z C E W C D U F I E O M M T L V S D A F
S U T H E R L A N D C S E S R O H E Y E
T U D N M P A V A R O T T I H A S W A P
```

METROPOLITAN	**OPERA HOUSE**	**LUCIANO**	**PAVAROTTI**
SKYROCKET	**TO STARDOM**	**COVENT**	**GARDEN**
SUTHERLAND	**AUSTRALIAN**	**SUCCESS**	**TELECAST LIVE**
TERRACOTTA	**ARMY**	**WARRIORS**	**HORSES**
FIRST EMPEROR	**ALL MADE**	**BY HAND**	**THOUSANDS**
LIFE SIZE	**FACE EAST**	**ARCHERS**	**CHARIOTS**

FILMS IN THE 70s - 1

1970 - 1974

1970 Love Story, was the biggest grossing film a sentimental, tearjerker with the oft-quoted tagline, "Love means never having to say you're sorry." Nominated for the Academy Awards Best Picture, it was beaten by **Patton** which won 7 major titles that year.

1971 The Oscar winner was **The French Connection** with Gene Hackman as a New York police detective, Jimmy 'Popeye' Doyle, chasing down drug smugglers. Hackman was at the peak of his career in the 70's.

1972 Francis Ford Coppola's gangster saga, **The Godfather** became the highest grossing film of its time and helped drive a resurgence in the American film industry.

1973 Glenda Jackson won Best Actress for her role in **A Touch of Class.** She revealed that she was approached for the part by the director after appearing in the 1971 'Antony & Cleopatra' sketch on the Morecambe & Wise show. After she won, Eric Morecambe sent her a telegram saying, "Stick with us and we will get you another one".

1974 New films this year included **The Godfather Part II,** which won the Oscar, **Blazing Saddles** the comedy western and the disaster film, **The Towering Inferno** starring Paul Newman and Steve McQueen.

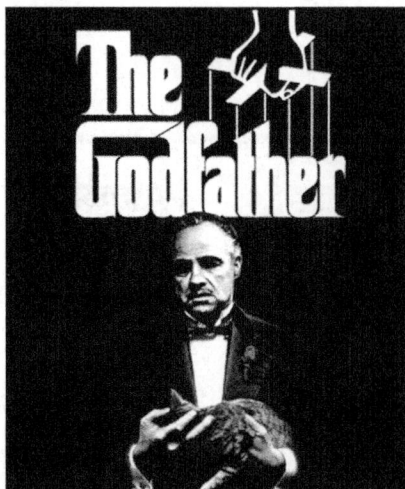

1975 - 1979

1975 One Flew Over the Cuckoo's Nest, an allegorical film set in a mental hospital, starring Jack Nicholson, beat tough competition for Best Picture from Spielberg's **Jaws** and Altman's **Nashville.**

1976 Jodi Foster won an Oscar in Martin Scorsese's gritty film **Taxi Driver** which examines alienation in urban society but it was Sylvester Stallone's **Rocky** that carried off the Best Picture award.

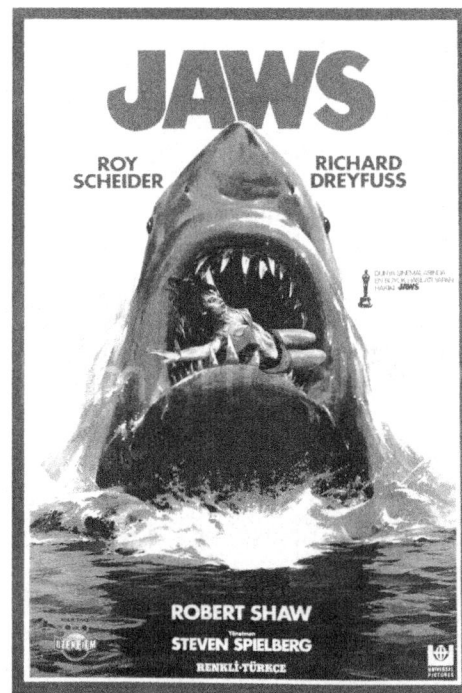

1977 Annie Hall from Woody Allen, the winner of Best Picture is a masterpiece of witty and quotable one-liners.

1978 The Vietnam War is examined through the lives of three friends from a small steel-mill town before, during and after their service in **The Deer Hunter**. A powerful and disturbing film.

1979 In this year's Best Picture, **Kramer v Kramer** there is a restaurant scene where Dustin Hoffman throws his wine glass at the wall. Only the cameraman was forewarned, Meryl Streep's shocked reaction was genuine!

```
J  I  F  R  E  N  C  H  Y  R  D  Z  A  T  R
K  O  C  Q  O  P  Q  Y  R  J  C  M  J  C  E
Z  M  O  V  N  P  X  K  O  X  K  O  A  R  T
R  I  X  N  R  G  A  C  T  K  H  R  W  E  N
E  R  V  B  E  T  N  O  S  A  N  E  S  H  U
V  N  B  W  F  W  D  R  E  F  B  C  A  T  H
I  A  A  Z  N  R  W  T  V  Z  Q  O  S  A  R
R  M  A  I  I  S  I  K  O  T  B  M  T  F  E
D  F  S  D  G  P  S  S  L  N  G  B  O  D  E
I  F  G  N  I  R  E  W  O  T  E  E  W  O  D
X  O  M  V  R  Y  L  Y  R  E  M  W  N  G  V
A  H  C  U  C  K  O  O  P  H  W  G  L  L  X
T  C  O  N  N  E  C  T  I  O  N  Z  N  I  V
P  E  E  R  T  S  K  Q  L  Z  S  Z  R  K  F
R  E  Z  K  D  M  R  Y  J  H  J  P  U  Y  I
```

LOVE STORY	FRENCH	CONNECTION	GODFATHER
MORECOMBE	AND WISE	TOWERING	INFERNO
CUCKOO	JAWS	ROCKY	TAXI DRIVER
DEER HUNTER	HOFFMAN	MERYL	STREEP

Star Wars

Star Wars all began with George Lucas's eponymous film in 1977. The epic space fantasy, telling the adventures of characters "A long time ago in a galaxy far, far away", and this first film was a world beater in special effects technology using new computerised and digital effects. It rapidly became a phenomenon, Luke Skywalker, Jedi Knights, Princess Leia and Darth Vader becoming household names. An immensely valuable franchise grew up to include the films, television series, video games, books, comics and theme parks which now amounts to billions of dollars and the film introduced the phrase "May the Force be with you" into common usage.

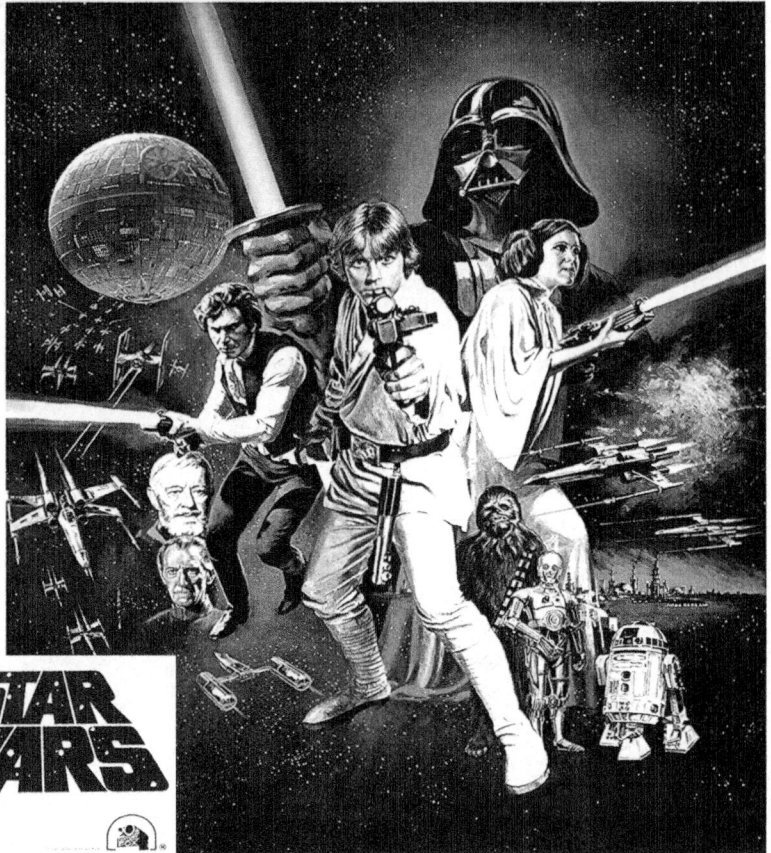

TWENTIETH CENTURY-FOX Presents A LUCASFILM LTD PRODUCTION STAR WARS
Starring MARK HAMILL HARRISON FORD CARRIE FISHER
PETER CUSHING
and
ALEC GUINNESS
Written and Directed by   Produced by   Music by
GEORGE LUCAS   GARY KURTZ   JOHN WILLIAMS
PANAVISION® PRINTS BY DE LUXE® TECHNICOLOR®

Making Films Sound Better
DOLBY SYSTEM
Noise Reduction · High Fidelity

Apocalypse Now

Joseph Conrad's book 'Heart of Darkness' was the inspiration for producer and director Francis Ford Coppola's psychological film, a metaphor for the madness and folly of war itself for a generation of young American men. Beautiful, with symbolic shots showing the confusion, violence and fear of the nightmare of the Vietnam War, much of it was filmed on location in the Philippines where expensive sets were destroyed by severe weather, a typhoon called 'Olga', Marlon Brando showed up on set overweight and completely unprepared and Martin Sheen had a near-fatal heart attack.

This led to the film being two and a half times over budget and taking twice the number of scheduled weeks to shoot. When filming finally finished, the release was postponed several times as Coppola had six hours of film to edit. The helicopter attack scene with the 'Ride of the Valkyries' soundtrack is one of the most memorable film scenes ever.

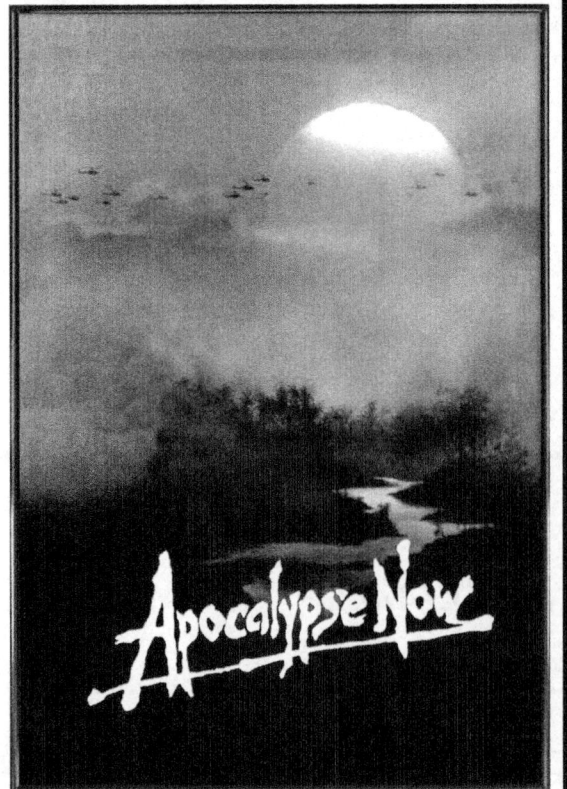

FILMS IN THE 70s - HARDER

```
E  T  J  R  C  B  R  A  W  M  A  N  T  E  I  V  R  A  V  Q
W  H  A  B  S  O  N  L  U  K  E  S  K  Y  W  A  L  K  E  R
F  N  I  A  W  C  P  P  A  M  K  I  C  I  L  O  B  M  Y  S
N  A  E  Q  E  L  T  P  R  P  V  T  F  P  C  V  J  H  G  E
F  C  L  W  I  T  H  Y  O  U  X  J  X  F  H  M  Q  W  S  S
O  I  S  G  R  S  Y  K  P  L  P  T  R  T  V  H  F  P  D  H
L  R  S  J  L  T  S  H  P  W  A  E  R  H  F  N  Y  S  Q  I
L  E  E  S  E  A  D  Q  M  Z  D  A  Y  A  O  L  D  D  G  X
Y  M  C  B  X  D  G  B  F  A  D  E  N  A  A  C  Z  Y  H  S
O  A  N  Q  N  X  I  P  V  W  T  T  P  C  W  R  L  M  H  E
F  G  I  P  C  Q  E  K  P  B  A  R  O  Z  Z  A  M  H  W  I
W  H  R  F  Z  R  E  P  N  S  H  P  O  Q  M  U  R  P  F  R
A  S  P  F  N  V  E  S  Y  I  A  H  Z  D  D  X  S  A  T  Y
R  E  O  O  Y  U  G  E  M  G  E  P  H  N  E  T  K  F  K
X  J  E  R  W  N  N  Y  G  F  P  H  H  I  W  A  A  V  M  L
S  P  E  C  I  A  L  O  X  R  F  I  T  X  M  H  R  I  A  A
T  S  A  E  Q  P  C  A  L  A  O  E  B  S  U  A  W  B  R  V
J  Z  Q  B  G  H  X  M  B  Q  L  E  C  J  K  Y  A  A  L  Y
R  X  B  E  Z  U  P  F  Q  D  H  A  G  T  A  B  R  Q  O  O
W  L  U  C  A  S  W  K  S  E  Z  K  G  Q  S  R  S  T  N  T
```

STAR WARS	GEORGE	LUCAS	FANTASY
GALAXY	FAR AWAY	SPECIAL	EFFECTS
LUKE SKYWALKER	JEDI KNIGHTS	PRINCESS LEIA	DARTH
VADER	FORCE BE	WITH YOU	APOCALYPSE
FOLLY OF WAR	AMERICAN	SYMBOLIC	VIETNAM WAR
MARLON	BRANDO	COPPOLA	VALKYRIES

Women Wear the Trousers

It is often said that 1970s styles had no direction and were too prolific. French couture no longer handed down diktats of what we should be wearing, and the emerging street style was inventive, comfortable, practical for women or glamorous. It could be home-made, it was whatever you wanted it to be, and the big new trend was for gender neutral clothes, women wore trousers in every walk of life, trouser suits for the office, jeans at home and colourful, tight-fitting ones for in between. Trouser legs became wider and 'bell-bottoms', flared from the knee down, with bottom leg openings of up to twenty-six inches, made from denim, bright cotton and satin polyester, became mainstream. Increasingly 'low cut', they were teamed with platform soles or high cut boots until they could not flare anymore, and so, by the end of the decade they had gone, skin-tight trousers, in earth tones, greys, whites and blacks were much more in vogue.

And the Hot Pants

In the early 70s, women's styles were very flamboyant with extremely bright colours and, in the winter, long, flowing skirts and trousers *but* come the summer, come the Hot Pants. These extremely short shorts were made of luxury fabrics such as velvet and satin designed for fashionable wear, not the practical equivalents for sports or leisure, and they enjoyed great popularity until falling out of fashion in the middle of the decade. Teamed with skin-tight t-shirts, they were favourites for clubwear and principally worn by women, including Jacqueline Kennedy Onassis, Elizabeth Taylor and Jane Fonda, but they were also worn by some high-profile men, David Bowie, Sammy Davis Jnr and Liberace among them, although the shorts were slightly longer than the women's versions, but still shorter than usual. Chest hair, medallions, sideburns and strangely, tennis headbands, finished the look!

70s Fashion - Easier

```
R C U G B L T H G I T N I K S
W J O N H M O T T O B L L E B
D X H O J J L S N E Q K G P L
U L Y S R E S U O R T E B L Q
Q F L A M B O Y A N T N E A F
L I W B E S E V W W G N E T L
A Q B B H O U P J L Z E N F O
S B N Z T L I O S R M D I O W
J C E J E E G H U E Z Y L R I
N X M J R S J U J G B N E M N
C D O H O T P A N T S M U V G
R O W A W F L A R E D R Q I R
F R A K L O W C U T O X C N K
S W N P E I W O B V R F A B A
U X R A E W B U L C T M J X P
```

WOMEN	**WORE THE**	**TROUSERS**	**FLARED**
BELL BOTTOM	**LOW CUT**	**PLATFORM**	**SOLES**
SKIN TIGHT	**HOT PANTS**	**FLAMBOYANT**	**FLOWING**
CLUBWEAR	**JACQUELINE**	**KENNEDY**	**BOWIE**

These Boots Are Made For Walking

Boots were so popular in the early 1970s that even men were getting in on the action. It wasn't uncommon to see a man sporting 2" inch platform boots inspired by John Travolta in Saturday Night Fever. The trend was all about being sexy on the dance floor!

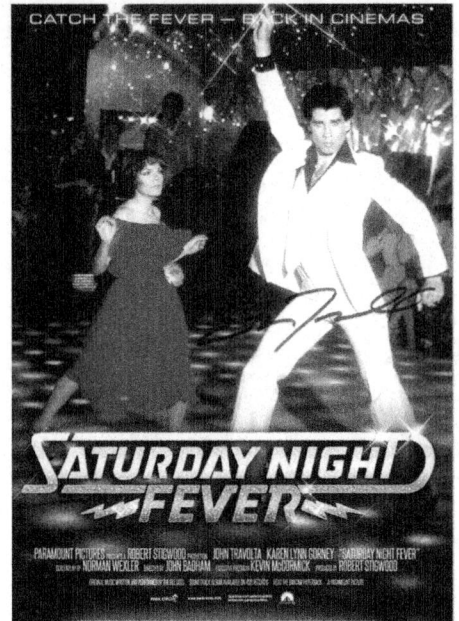

And Punk Was Not to Be Ignored

Emerging in the mid 70s in London as an anarchic and aggressive movement, a few hundred young people defined themselves as an anti-fashion urban youth street culture closely aligned to the music that became punk. They cut up old clothes from charity shops, destroyed the fabric and refashioned outfits in a manner intended to shock. Trousers were deliberately torn to reveal laddered tights and dirty legs and worn with heavy Doc Martens footwear, now seen on many young women too.

Safety pins and chains held bits of fabric together. Neck chains were made from padlocks and chain and even razor blades were used as pendants. Body piercings and studs, beginning with the three-stud earlobe, progressing to the ear outline embedded with ear studs, evolved to pins in eyebrows, cheeks, noses or lips and together with tattoos were the beginning of unisex fashion. All employed by male and female alike to offend. Vivienne Westwood and Malcolm McLaren quickened the style with her bondage shop "Sex", and his punk music group, the "Sex Pistols".

```
G T S G N I C R E I P P T I G H T S E
B W V T R O F E D A M S G M Z E T R K E
C T R S K C O L D A P Y N K U B O Z K F
O O Z A M R T S K F R E V E F O V B R K
S S O J N W M E O L A D A Z L F S N G Z
N V R F K M V X S D E O E F R A N P B J
E G K U X D X Y Y N X V E R T A U L A I
T C D M R Q C O D Z I C I U A N X N U Y
R H E Z N Y R N R E N P R S K S A V P D
A A R Z H S H D O A N D Y R S R T A R I
M R E J M E B J D Z A U O T C E B O K M
C I D Q P K J J I Y R C C H E U R F O F
O T D J C N G W Z Z K B I P U F J G P B
D Y A C N Q Z E D B M C O T B Z A B G J
Y S L N I G H T G S T R E E T A H S G A
D H N G N I K L A W H A M R O F T A L P
J O G H V A J Z Y C U L T U R E W X F L
T P D B H L B W C M A T L O V A R T H P
G S B T N S K R W Y Y O U T H U S M B W
R S I S W Q B F U R Y L J P V Q N Y G I
```

BOOTS ARE	MADE FOR	WALKING	PLATFORM
TRAVOLTA	SATURDAY	NIGHT	FEVER
SEXY ON	DANCE FLOOR	ANARCHIC	AGGRESSIVE
URBAN	YOUTH	STREET	CULTURE
CHARITY SHOPS	LADDERED	TIGHTS	DOC MARTENS
SAFETY PINS	PADLOCKS	PIERCINGS	PUNK ROCK

LEISURE IN THE 70s - 1

SATURDAY MORNING TV

In the early 70s, Saturday mornings for many children still meant a trip to the cinema but with the advent of Saturday Morning Television, under instruction 'not to wake their parents', children could creep downstairs, switch on the box and stay entertained until lunchtime.

First, in 1974, came ITV's 'Tiswas', hosted by Chris Tarrant it was a chaotic blend of jokes, custard pies and buckets of water.

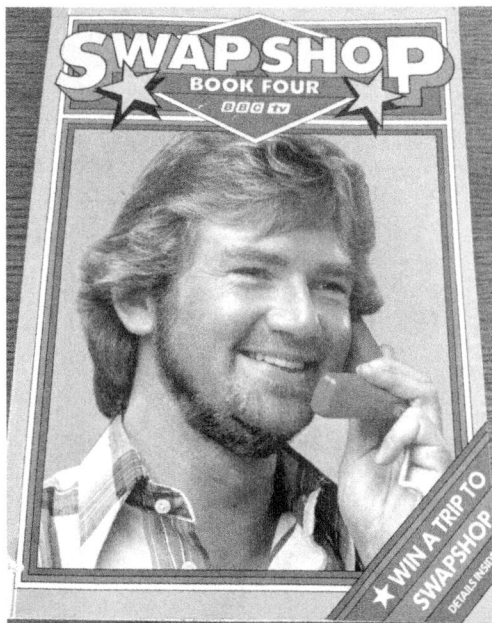

Then in 1976, the BBC introduced 'Swap Shop' with Noel Edmonds, Keith Chegwin and John Craven and a Saturday morning ritual was born. Nearly three hours of ground-breaking television using the 'phone-in' extensively for the first time on TV. The programme included music, competitions, cartoons and spontaneous nonsense from Edmonds. There was coverage of news and issues relevant to children, presented by 'Newsround's' John Craven but by far the most popular element of the show was the "Swaporama" open-air event, hosted by Chegwin. An outside broadcast unit would travel to different locations throughout the UK where sometimes as many as 2000 children would gather to swap their belongings with others.

SATURDAY NIGHT FEVER

Memories of Saturday night and Sunday morning in the discotheque. A mirror ball; strobe lights; 'four on the floor' rhythm; the throb of the bass drum; girls in Spandex tops with hot pants or vividly coloured, shiny, Lycra trousers with equally dazzling halter neck tops; boys in imitations of John Travolta's white suit from Saturday Night Fever risking life and limb on towering platform shoes.

These glamorous dancers, clad in glitter, metallic lame and sequins, gyrating as the music pounded out at the direction of the DJ, whirling energetically and glowing bright 'blue-white' under the ultra-violet lights as their owners 'strutted their stuff', perspiration running in rivulets down their backs.

The DJs, stars in their own right, mixed tracks by Donna Summer, the Bee Gees, Gloria Gaynor, Sister Sledge, Chic and Chaka Khan, as their sexy followers, fuelled by the night club culture of alcohol and drugs, changed from dancing the Hustle with their partners to the solo freestyle dancing of John Travolta.

70s Leisure - Easier

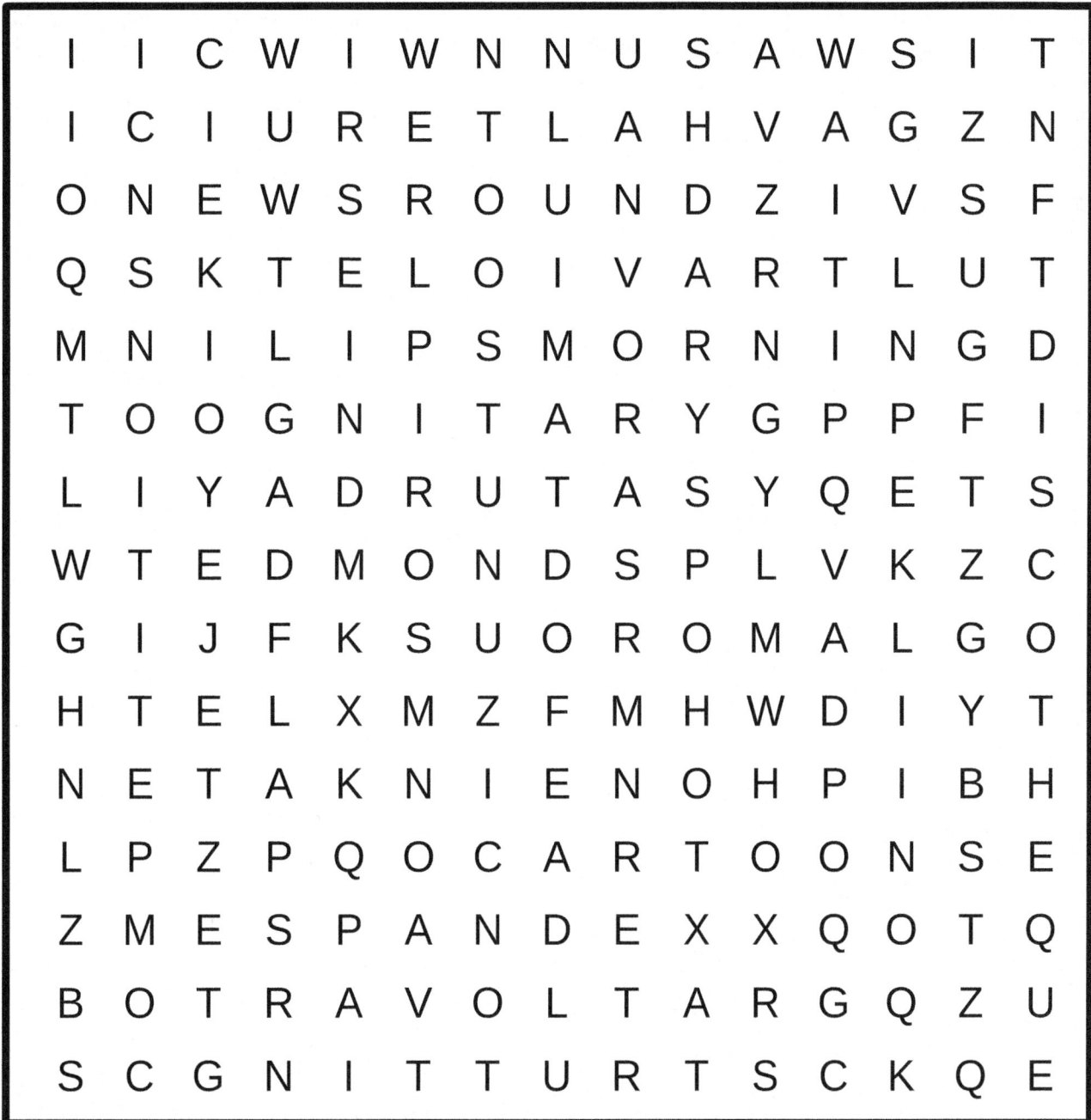

```
I I C W I W N N U S A W S I T
I C I U R E T L A H V A G Z N
O N E W S R O U N D Z I V S F
Q S K T E L O I V A R T L U T
M N I L I P S M O R N I N G D
T O O G N I T A R Y G P P F I
L I Y A D R U T A S Y Q E T S
W T E D M O N D S P L V K Z C
G I J F K S U O R O M A L G O
H T E L X M Z F M H W D I Y T
N E T A K N I E N O H P I B H
L P Z P Q O C A R T O O N S E
Z M E S P A N D E X X Q O T Q
B O T R A V O L T A R G Q Z U
S C G N I T T U R T S C K Q E
```

SATURDAY	MORNING	TISWAS	EDMONDS
PHONE IN	COMPETITIONS	CARTOONS	NEWSROUND
DISCOTHEQUE	SPANDEX	HALTER	TRAVOLTA
GLAMOROUS	GYRATING	ULTRA VIOLET	STRUTTING

THE DANGERS OF LEISURE

In the 1970's the Government was intent on keeping us all – and particularly children – safe and continued producing the wartime Public Information Films, which were still scaring children witless!

1971: Children and Disused Fridges: Graphic warnings of children being suffocated in old fridges that, tempted by their playful imaginations, they want to climb into.

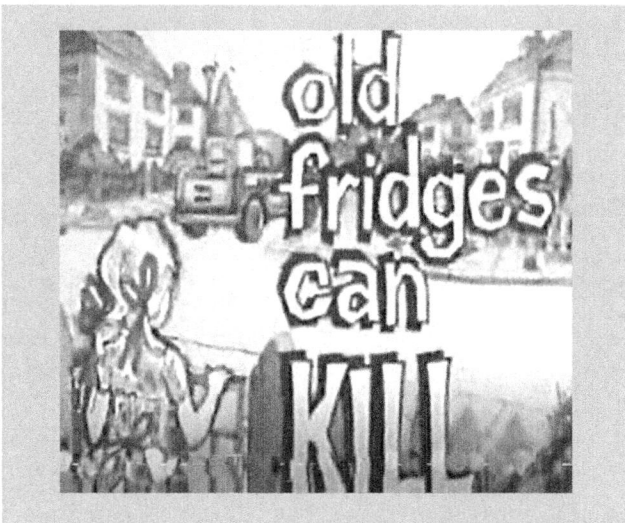

1973: Broken Glass: This film shows a boy running on the sand, ending abruptly before he steps on a broken glass bottle, the film urges people to use a bin or take their litter home with them.

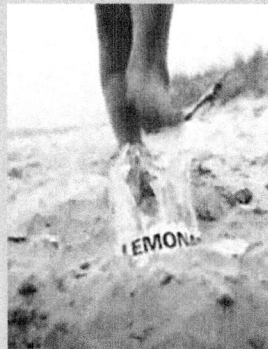

1974: The Fatal Floor: This 30 second film had the message, "Polish a floor, put a rug on it, and you might as well set a man trap…"

1979: Play Safe – Frisbee: This film used chilling electronic music and frightening sound effects to highlight the potentially fatal combination of frisbees with electricity pylons and kites, fishing rods and radio-controlled planes.

1972: Teenagers – Learn to Swim:

A cartoon aimed at teenagers warns them to learn how to swim, or risk social embarrassment and failure to attract the opposite sex. The female character's illusion of her boyfriend 'Dave' being able 'to do anything' is shattered after she wishes they were at the seaside, where she discovers Dave can't swim. He in turn wishes he didn't 'keep losing me birds' after his girlfriend disappears with 'Mike' who 'swims like a fish'. Although the film is light-hearted in tone it was intended in part to help prevent accidents.

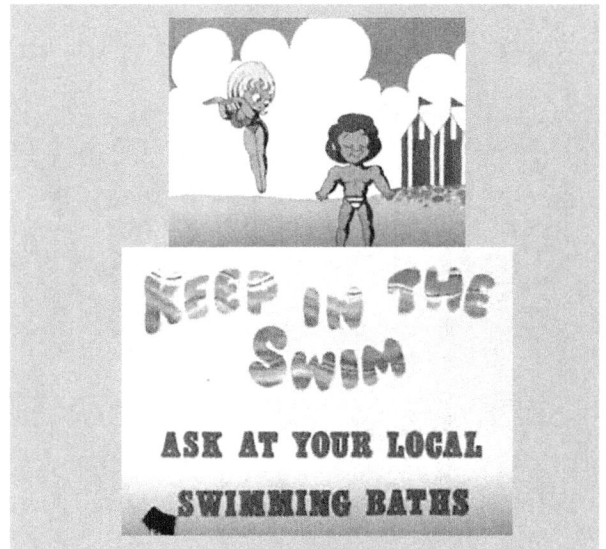

1975: Protect and Survive:

This was the title of a series of booklets and films made in the late 1970s and early 1980s, dealing with emergency planning for a nuclear war including the recognition of attack warning, fallout warning, and all-clear signals, the preparation of a home "fallout room" and the stockpiling of food, water, and other emergency supplies. In the opinion of some contemporary critics, the films *were deeply and surprisingly fatalistic in tone*!

70s Leisure - Harder

```
X M U P W P B R B O T T L E C E P M M X
N X L R U R C W K F A T A L H F F Z A S
L K R Q Y C L X S J F V Q H W M U N E V
V T R M B C P I F T F O F R I S B E E H
Q A I F E P N G N A E N S V W C G H V O
B R O K E N R E L O Z L Y R X V N U W L
Q Z E Y P A Y L G N I P K S E Q I J E S
N D M S P M O K Y R B T M O O G N E T E
F H S H V U A B W K E L A K O Y N A B G
Y B I D T A P D B I I M S M O B A A Y D
M C S O Z V I E Z F A F E G R H L F D I
M E L E D S H R L Z I L I L Q O P T L R
C W D F U N H U Y C X O S T A X F H M F
A F L S R H R S N B O O L C G A J N B A
D V E A M Z J I T H J R N V F E P X I G
G D E C V H V E Y T I C I R T C E L E L
A L R P E V U L D X Z C L F F S X Q M A
W A R N I N G S X R A W R A E L C U N S
M L F G N I L I P K C O T S E U N X M S
M I W S O T H W Y L L A I T N E T O P E
```

DANGERS OF	LEISURE	INFORMATION	FILMS
DISUSED	FRIDGES	GRAPHIC	WARNINGS
BROKEN	GLASS	BOTTLE	FATAL FLOOR
FRISBEE	POTENTIALLY	FATAL	ELECTRICITY
LEARN	TO SWIM	BOOKLETS	EMERGENCY
PLANNING	NUCLEAR WAR	FALLOUT	STOCKPILING

MUSIC IN THE 70s - 1

1970 - 1974

1970 Number 1 for 3 weeks, **Bridge Over Troubled Water** by Simon and Garfunkel became their 'signature song' selling over 6m copies worldwide. It also became one of the most performed songs of the 20th century, covered by over 50 artists.

1971 George Harrison's first release as a solo **My Sweet Lord** topped the charts for five weeks and became the best selling UK single of the year.
Rod Stewart had 7 No 1's this year including in October, the double sided hits, **Reason to Believe/Maggie May**

1972 A jingle, rewritten to become the hugely popular 'Buy the world a Coke' advert for the Coca Cola company, was re-recorded by The New Seekers as the full-length song, **I'd Like to Teach the World to Sing**, which stayed at No 1 for 4 weeks.

1973 Dawn featuring Tony Orlando had the bestselling single of 1973 with **"Tie a Yellow Ribbon Round the 'Ole Oak Tree"**, which spent four weeks at the top spot and lasted 11 weeks in the top ten.
Queen released their debut album, **"Queen"**. The Carpenters reached number 2 with **"Yesterday Once More"**.

1974 Waterloo, the winning song for Sweden in the Eurovision Song Contest began ABBA's journey to world-wide fame.
David Essex has his first No 1 with **Wanna Make You a Star** which spends 3 weeks at the top of the charts.

1975 - 1979

1975 Make Me Smile (Come Up and See Me) was a chart topper for Steve Harley & Cockney Rebel. **Bohemian Rhapsody** for Queen, stayed at the top for nine weeks.

1976 The Brotherhood of Man won the Eurovision Song Contest for Great Britain with **Save Your Kisses for Me**. It became the biggest-selling song of the year and remains one of the biggest-selling Eurovision winners ever.
Don't Go Breaking My Heart was the first No. 1 single in the UK for both Elton John and Kiki Dee.

1977 Actor David Soul, riding high on his success in Starsky & Hutch, had the No 1 spot for 4 weeks with **Don't Give Up on Us**.
Way Down was the last song to be recorded by Elvis Presley before his death and stayed at No 1 for 5 weeks.

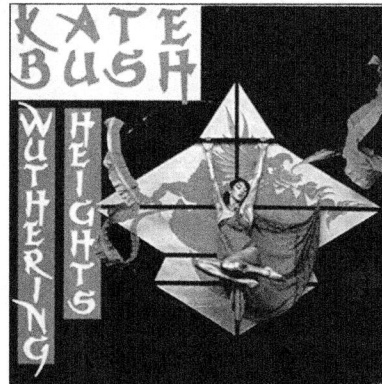

1978 Kate Bush released her debut single, **Wuthering Heights,** which she had written aged 18 after watching Emily Brontë's Wuthering Heights on television and discovering she shared the author's birthday.
Spending five weeks at the top of the British charts, Boney M's **"Rivers of Babylon"** became the biggest selling single of the year, exceeding one million sales between May and June.

1979 Frequently recalled as a symbol of female empowerment, **I Will Survive** reached the top for Gloria Gaynor.
The Wall, Pink Floyd's rock opera was released, featuring all three parts of **Another Brick in the Wall. Part 2**, written as a protest against rigid schooling was No1 in Dec.

MUSIC IN THE 70s - EASIER

```
W  T  F  Y  E  L  L  O  W  V  T  C  X  E  U
D  M  W  E  N  E  H  T  Z  F  L  D  N  K  K
O  R  A  K  O  Y  S  O  F  C  V  K  H  T  N
V  U  T  P  O  E  E  E  X  C  C  U  O  Q  K
T  G  E  R  B  L  E  U  T  K  U  S  J  B  O
R  C  R  J  H  S  K  R  S  H  M  T  N  W  Y
O  S  L  E  N  E  E  O  R  S  N  A  O  G  I
U  W  O  G  O  R  R  V  E  U  E  R  T  A  F
B  N  O  D  B  P  S  I  T  B  E  S  L  R  L
L  J  T  I  B  S  I  S  N  E  U  K  E  F  K
E  Z  M  R  I  I  Z  I  E  T  Q  Y  T  U  N
D  C  G  B  R  V  M  O  P  A  D  V  P  N  D
D  R  W  S  P  L  B  N  R  K  Q  H  L  K  J
O  X  S  E  Q  E  Z  O  A  B  W  D  O  E  J
B  V  R  E  V  O  B  E  C  V  Y  V  N  L  W
```

BRIDGE OVER	**TROUBLED**	**WATERS**	**GARFUNKEL**
THE NEW	**SEEKERS**	**YELLOW**	**RIBBON**
QUEEN	**CARPENTERS**	**WATERLOO**	**EUROVISION**
ELTON JOHN	**STARSKY**	**ELVIS PRESLEY**	**KATE BUSH**

ABBA
THANK YOU FOR THE MUSIC

THE DECADE IN NUMBERS

Most No1 Singles:
ABBA with seven.
Waterloo (1974);
Mamma Mia, Fernando
and
Dancing Queen (all 1976);
**Knowing Me Knowing You,
The Name of the Game,**
(both 1977);
Take a Chance on Me
(1978).

Most Weeks at No 1:
Bohemian Rhapsody by
Queen; **Mull of Kintyre /
Girl's School** by Wings;
You're the One That I Want
by John Travolta and Olivia
Newton-John.

ABBA Waterloo

BOHEMIAN
RHAPSODY

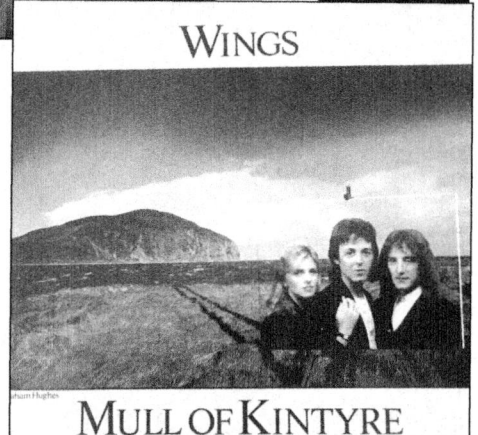

WINGS

MULL OF KINTYRE

'Danny' and 'Sandy' Fever

Grease, the 1978 musical romantic comedy starring John Travolta (Danny) and Olivia Newton-John (Sandy) had phenomenal success. In June to August 1978, **You're the One That I Want** and in September to October, **Summer Nights**, locked up the number 1 position for a total of sixteen weeks.

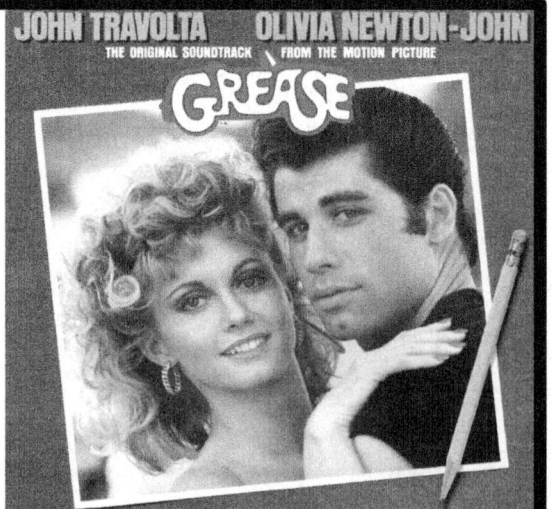

THE ORIGINAL MOVIE SOUND TRACK
SATURDAY NIGHT FEVER
STEREO 2658 123

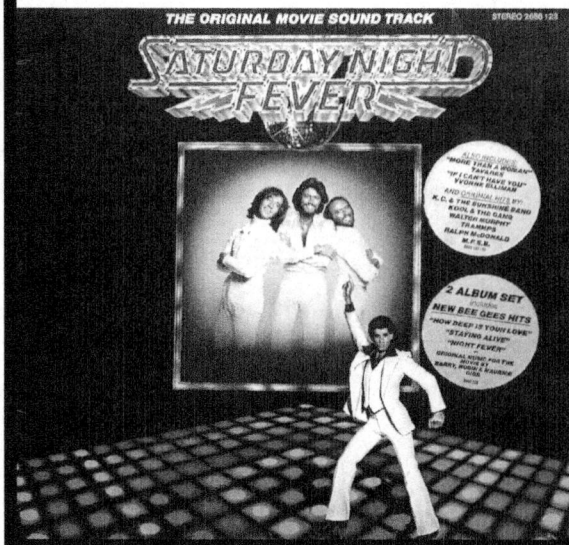

JOHN TRAVOLTA   OLIVIA NEWTON-JOHN
THE ORIGINAL SOUNDTRACK   FROM THE MOTION PICTURE
GREASE

Hopelessly Devoted to You was nominated for an Oscar and John Travolta and Olivia Newton-John seemed to be constantly in the public conscience. Critically and commercially successful, the soundtrack album ended 1978 as the second best-selling album in the US, behind the soundtrack of the 1977 blockbuster **Saturday Night Fever,** which also starred John Travolta.

MUSIC IN THE 70s - HARDER

```
B T T K N O W I N G M E K O J V C Q P I
T D L W I E O Z F I R R Q A N T N N H S
Z K E Y D O S P A H R L M T F E W X E R
S U Z C R E V E F T H G I N W G A B N R
O Q H Y A D R U T A S B M T E S T D O F
U N K Y A E K A T S Y R O I I U E C M C
N Q Z W T V Q C A N Z N Y Q G C R L E M
D A R H P O Q E P S J A B Q J C L S N A
T T D B S W D C M O H F N D U E O J A M
R L U R L P Q H A S Q Q A G S O C L M
A O B M Z O I N A A G X F Y I S G Y R A
C V Y T O L C B D J N E D I K M L F L M
K A A N L N B K N E R C H P E W E A R I
F R B A I A E N B N Z U E T H L D H J A
Q T T W V D C E A U Z N R O F Z A O O K
Z N H I I T W N U Y S J E M N O N F G B
W H E T A F D A J Q G T J M H J C A K B
J O O A C O D C C B E Q E U A V I F G G
T J N H K C M V N O M F O R X N N E D N
A A E T F C Q T G A D I Q Z D U G Y L Y
```

ABBA	WATERLOO	MAMMA MIA	FERNANDO
DANCING	QUEEN	KNOWING ME	THE NAME
OF THE GAME	TAKE A	CHANCE ON ME	BOHEMIAN
RHAPSODY	JOHN TRAVOLTA	OLIVIA	NEWTON JOHN
PHENOMENAL	SUCCESS	THE ONE	THAT I WANT
SATURDAY	NIGHT FEVER	SOUNDTRACK	BLOCKBUSTER

Pocket Calculators

The first pocket calculators came onto the market towards the end of 1970. In the early 70s they were an expensive status symbol but by the middle of the decade, businessmen were quite used to working their sales figures out quickly whilst 'out of the office'.

Household accounts were made easy and children wished they could use them at school – not just to help with homework. Most early calculators performed only basic addition, subtraction, multiplication and division but the speed and accuracy, sometimes giving up to 12 digit answers, of the machine proved sensational.

In 1972, Hewlett Packard introduced the revolutionary HP-35 pocket calculator which, in addition to the basic operations, enabled advanced mathematical functions. It was the first scientific, hand-held calculator, able to perform a wide number of logarithmic and trigonometric functions, store intermediate solutions and utilise scientific notations.

With intense competition, prices of pocket calculators dropped rapidly, and the race was on to produce the smallest possible models. The target was to be no bigger than a credit card. Casio won the race.

The Miracle of IVF

In 1971, Patrick Steptoe, gynaecologist, Robert Edwards, biologist, and Jean Purdy, nurse and embryologist set up a small laboratory at the Kershaw's Hospice in Oldham which was to lead to the development of in vitro fertilisation and eventual birth of Louise Brown in 1978.

They developed a technique for retrieving eggs at the right time and fertilising them in the laboratory, believing that they could be implanted back in the uterus. It took more than 80 embryo transfers before the first successful pregnancy, and the birth of Louise, the first 'test-tube baby', heralded the potential happiness of infertile people and a bright future for British science and industry. 8

```
H O G D V D E C N A V D A Y M
B F U N C T I O N S D U C U A
X T R A N S F E R V I J T W T
T R C A L C U L A T O R S T H
A R M X N O I T A T O N L N E
F T T E L W E H C B P C F A M
P X U U K W P Y I Q Q I D B A
O Y R B M E P I F U N H R Q T
C Z B C U S J C I H I N A S I
K B A Z F M M O T C X Z K U C
E M B F Q J N J N D I W C T A
T S Y E V I S N E P X E A A L
S Y M B O L T J I D W Y P T U
U S T L M I Z L C T I A B S S
E B U T T S E T S A W F Z A A
```

POCKET	CALCULATORS	EXPENSIVE	STATUS
SYMBOL	HEWLETT	PACKARD	ADVANCED
FUNCTIONS	MATHEMATICAL	SCIENTIFIC	NOTATION
TEST TUBE	BABY	EMBRYO	TRANSFER

SCIENCE AND NATURE - 2

"Houston We Have a Problem"

In April 1970, two days after the launch of Apollo 13, the seventh crewed mission in the Apollo space program and the third meant to land on the Moon, the NASA ground crew heard the now famous message, "Houston, we've had a problem." An oxygen tank had exploded, and the lunar landing was aborted leaving the astronauts in serious danger. The crew looped around the Moon and returned safely to Earth, their safe return being down to the ingenuity under pressure by the crew, commanded by Jim Lovell, together with the flight controllers and mission control. The crew experienced great hardship, caused by limited power, a chilly and wet cabin and a shortage of drinking water.

Even so, Apollo 13 set a spaceflight record for the furthest humans have travelled from Earth.

Tens of millions of viewers watched Apollo 13 splashdown in the South Pacific Ocean and the recovery by USS Iwo Jima.

The global campaigning network **Greenpeace** was founded in 1971 by Irving and Dorothy Stowe, environmental activists. The network now has 26 independent national or regional organisations in 55 countries worldwide.

Their stated goal is to ensure the ability of the earth to nurture life in all its diversity. To achieve this they "use non-violent, creative confrontation to expose global environmental problems, and develop solutions for a green and peaceful future". In detail to:

- Stop the planet from warming beyond 1.5° in order to prevent the most catastrophic impacts of the climate breakdown.
- Protect biodiversity in all its forms.
- Slow the volume of hyper-consumption and learn to live within our means.
- Promote renewable energy as a solution that can power the world.
- Nurture peace, global disarmament and non-violence.

SCIENCE & NATURE - HARDER

```
D N F V G U Q U P B K B O Q R Z G O H N
B O E D A E V A H E W B H O U S T O N U
W O I D E W O V E J U U P C J T F A O C
V M V S E T S A S T R O N A U T S P C I
J E E V B D R E G E R A N U L Z B F G D
N H E C W R O O N Y D N Q N I B I Q I A
B T C T A W N L B E H R C J E N O A W N
B P P O A E A M P A R C U Q C S D C Y G
P Q E Q G M P P M X F G S W A S I T D E
Z Z X Y D G I N O X E X Y H E I V I O R
C C X N A Y P L E L R R O H P N E V E N
N O J O D Z Z X C E L V J E V F R I S V
N W O D H S A L P S R O S Z O Q S S T M
P A S E R I O U S D H G B A J K I T W N
I V R A S C R E C O V E R Y F M T S R O
V L E N V I R O N M E N T A L X Y E Z D
H J S X U T H C M M E L B O R P A P I N
E P G I U Z G N I D N A L U N Z E G F A
G B H P A N R E N E W A B L E J S Z K L
K G Y D W K J V B C P Z C A U D T W D A
```

HOUSTON	WE HAVE A	PROBLEM	APOLLO
LAND ON	THE MOON	OXYGEN	EXPLODED
LUNAR	LANDING	ABORTED	ASTRONAUTS
SERIOUS	DANGER	SPLASHDOWN	RECOVERY
GREENPEACE	ENVIRONMENTAL	ACTIVISTS	CLIMATE
BIODIVERSITY	RENEWABLE	ENERGY	PEACE

SPORT IN THE 70s - 1

1970 - 1974

1970 The thoroughbred 'Nijinsky', wins all three English Triple Crown Races: **The 2,000 Guineas** at Newmarket; **The Derby** at Epsom; the **St. Leger Stakes** at Doncaster and the Irish Derby. The first horse to do this in 35 years and not repeated as of 2021.

1971 Arsenal wins both the **First Division** title and the **FA Cup**, becoming the fourth team ever to win the double.
Jack Nicklaus wins his ninth major at the **PGA Championship**, the first golfer ever to win all four majors for the second time.

1972 At **Wimbledon**, Stan Smith (US) beat Ilie Nastase in the Men's Singles Final. It was his only Wimbledon title.
In the Women's Final, Billie Jean King (US) beat Yvonne Goolagong (AUS) to gain her fourth **Wimbledon** title.
The **Olympic Games** held in Munich are overshadowed by the murder of eleven Israeli athletes and coaches by Palestinian Black September members.

1973 George Foreman knocks out Joe Frazier in only two rounds to take the **World Heavyweight Boxing** Championship title.

Red Rum wins the **Grand National** with a new record and staging a spectacular comeback on the run-in having trailed the leader by 15 lengths at the final fence.

1974 Liverpool win the **FA Cup Final** against Newcastle United at Wembley. Kevin Keegan scored two of their three goals.
Eddie Merckx wins the **Tour de France**, becoming the first rider to win the Triple Crown of Cycling, **Tour de France**, **Giro d'Italia** and **World Championships** in one calendar year.

1975 - 1979

1975 In athletics, John Walker (NZ) sets a new world record becoming the first man to **run a mile** in under 3 mins 50 seconds. He clocks 3mins 49.4 secs.
Muhammad Ali defeats Joe Frazier in the 'Thrilla In Manilla' to maintain the **Boxing Heavyweight Championship** of the world.

1976 The **Olympics** are held in Montreal. Britain's only medal is a Bronze, won by Brendan Foster running the **10,000 metres**.
John Curry, becomes the **European, Olympic and World Figure Skating Champion**. He was the first skater to combine, ballet and modern dance into his skating.

1977 The commercial **World Series Cricket** was introduced by Kerry Packer. WSC changed the nature of the game with its emphasis on the "gladiatorial" aspect of fast bowling and heavy promotion of fast bowlers.

1978 During the **Oxford and Cambridge Boat Race,** the Cambridge boat sinks. It is the first sinking in the race since 1951.
Wales wins the rugby **Five Nations Championship** and completes the Grand Slam having beaten England, France, Ireland and Scotland.

1978 Arsenal beat Manchester United 3-2 in the **FA Cup Final.**
At **The Open** at Royal Lytham & St Annes Golf Club Seve Ballesteros becomes the first golfer from Continental Europe to win a major since 1907.

70s Sport - Easier

```
U X K J O H N C U R R Y L D G
T M B O A T R A C E B N O X H
P J W H C P Y R Y O A O O X G
G H A P D P K E X X L D P K J
C U L E M R S I S F L E R S U
I V E S B M N Z U O E L E A A
B W S A M U I A A R S B V R S
V D O T U N J R L D T M I S G
E Z H S R I I F K L E I L E D
C L W A D C N E C Q R W A N X
V E A N E H V O I H O Q X A V
G I T H R Y T J N F S N D L X
E N T A X K C R E M Z B W N G
T T W V V J J P Q X F R K N B
B R M N A M E R O F H L P J V
```

NIJINSKY	ARSENAL	NICKLAUS	WIMBLEDON
NASTASE	MUNICH	FOREMAN	RED RUM
LIVERPOOL	MERCKX	JOE FRAZIER	JOHN CURRY
BOAT RACE	OXFORD	WALES	BALLESTEROS

Traffic Lights and Football

Before the introduction of Red and Yellow Cards in football, cautions or sending a player off had to be dealt with orally, and the language barrier could sometimes present problems. For example, in the 1966 World Cup, the German referee tried in vain to send Argentinian player Antonio Rattin off the field, but Rattin did not 'want' to understand and eventually was escorted off the pitch by the police! Ken Aston, Head of World Cup Referees, was tasked with solving this problem and legend has it that the idea of the red and yellow cards came to him when he was stopped in his car at traffic lights. They were tested in the 1968 Olympics and the 1970 World Cup in Mexico and introduced to European leagues soon after and after six years, to English football.

In 1976, the first player to be sent off using a red card in an English game was Blackburn Rovers winger David Wagstaffe.

Tour de France

In 1974 the Tour de France covered 2,546 miles in 22 stages, one of which was the first to be held in the UK, a circuit stage on the Plympton By-pass near Plymouth. Eddy Merckx of Belgium won eight stages and won the race overall with a comfortable margin, making it five wins for him out of his five Tours. He also won that year's Combination Classification – the General (Yellow Jersey), Points or Sprint (Green Jersey) and Mountains (since 1975, King of the Mountains wears the Polka Dot Jersey).

Rockstar and Racing Driver

James Hunt, the charismatic, play-boy darling of the press in the 1970's, began his Formula 1 career at the beginning of the decade with the Hesketh Racing team and gave them their only win in 1975 at the Dutch GP. He moved to McLaren in 1976, and in his first year with them, he and his great rival Niki Lauda at Ferrari, fought an epic season-long battle. It was an extraordinarily dramatic season, over sixteen races filled with drama and controversy, where Lauda had gained an early championship lead. By the final race in Japan, he was being reeled-in by Hunt and was only three points ahead. Hunt drove the race of his life, in the worst possible weather conditions, to finish in third place. Lauda, already badly injured from the crash at Nürburgring in August, withdrew because of the hazardous conditions which meant James Hunt became World Champion, winning by just a single point.

Hunt's natural driving ability was phenomenal, and while his habit of risk-taking didn't always endear him to others, hence the nickname "Hunt the Shunt", it also made him compelling to watch. Off track, he and Niki had an enduring friendship, which lasted after James's retirement from F1 in 1979 until his untimely death from a heart attack in 1993, aged just 45.

70s Sport - Harder

```
Q E Y W N A I N I T N E G R A T N K S Y
P U C D L R O W I U H N R I T R I D K O
F G H D D X O N J E R S E Y E N G A M J
V F E L J V O F B K Z T X V G O A O D G
H O S A D U A L I K I N I O W Y M D B M
X R K D S D Q O C H C R F P X R R P H R
E M E G O U K S I G D T P V O E Q J F T
C U T A K E Z I R G H K K L F Z C A F O
N L H I Q M C R N E Z O Y E G X N M O D
A A S E C Q C I B R H M R M R I O E G A
R O N O O F C P M E P E N C R B T S N K
F N I N U A F N E I E J Q A T C P H I L
E E A O R M U L C S Q D R L I E M U D O
D J T I R A T S K C O R R F I B Y N N P
R Z N P Z M B W D K E E F A S R L T E X
U J U M W M R H A F S A A U C X P J S Z
O S O A X M E I H O R Q M F N D D D X A
T J M H Z U M W K T Z W G G M D E U C E
P T O C S W W S T H G I L M C L A R E N
Z Q K U U W E D D Y M E R C K X L X P I
```

RED CARD

SENDING OFF

ARGENTINIAN

REFEREES

TRAFFIC

LIGHTS

OLYMPICS

WORLD CUP

PLYMPTON

TOUR DE FRANCE

EDDY MERCKX

JERSEY

KING OF THE

MOUNTAINS

POLKA DOT

ROCKSTAR

FORMULA ONE

RACING DRIVER

JAMES HUNT

HESKETH

MCLAREN

NIKI LAUDA

FERRARI

CHAMPION

TRANSPORT IN THE 70s - 1

ICONIC MACHINES OF THE DECADE

The Jumbo Jet
Entered service on January 22, 1970. The 747 was the first airplane dubbed a "Jumbo Jet", the first wide-body airliner.

In 1971 Ford launched the car that was to represent the 1970s, the Cortina Mk III. In 1976 the Mk IV and 1979 Mk V. Cortinas were the best-selling cars of the decade.

The best-selling foreign import was the Datsun Sunny, which was only the 19th best-selling car of the decade.

In 1973, British Leyland's round, dumpy shaped Allegro was not at all popular and meagre sales contributed greatly to BL's collapse in 1975.

Raleigh Chopper
Shot to fame in the 70's when every child, and some adults, wanted one. It had a high back, long seat and motorbike rear wheel and was probably the first bike to have a centrally positioned gear shift.

```
M F P T V A I C O N I C K U Z
T A E S G N O L G F G G M J P
T W O L E K P S S P U V R I D
J N U S T A D I C N Q A K M I
W G N I L L E S T S E B S Z X
Y N N U S M A C H I N E S F N
G A H F T E J O B M U J F X D
E L A O Y D N G I E R O F U D
A L B M Q A V S N B P T I U Q
R E K V T C O R T I N A T D C
L G Y R I E B I M P O R T X Y
E R D I E D U P H G I E L A R
V O U M M F O T B B Y P M U D
E F T D S O Y L M A H B D F V
R C M V R E P P O H C G E Z F
```

ICONIC	**MACHINES**	**JUMBO JET**	**CORTINA**
BEST SELLING	**OF DECADE**	**FOREIGN**	**IMPORT**
DATSUN	**SUNNY**	**ALLEGRO**	**DUMPY**
RALEIGH	**CHOPPER**	**LONG SEAT**	**GEAR LEVER**

TRANSPORT IN THE 70s - 2

Women Drivers

In 1974, Jill Viner became the first female bus driver for London Transport. She trained to become a bus driver at a centre in Chiswick in 1974, when London Transport were said to be 3,200 drivers short

While women had previously driven buses within bus depots during the Second World War, Viner was the first women to drive a bus in service in London. In the weeks after she started driving, it was reported that thirty women had applied to become bus drivers.

In 1978, Hannah Dadds completed a seven-week training course to qualify as a train driver and became the first female driver on the London Underground.

Hannah's sister Edna also joined the London Underground working first as a guard and then a driver. Hannah and Edna became the first all-female crew on the London Underground.

Concorde

The Anglo-French supersonic passenger airliner had a take-off speed of 220 knots (250mph) and a cruising speed of 1350mph – more than twice the speed of sound. With seating for 92 to 128 passengers, Concorde entered service in 1976 and operated for 27 years.

Twenty aircraft were built in total, including six prototypes and in the end, only Air France and British Airways purchased and flew them, due in great part to supersonic flights being restricted to ocean-crossing routes, to prevent sonic boom disturbance over land and populated areas. Concorde flew regular transatlantic flights from London and Paris to New York, Washington, Dulles in Virginia and Barbados and the BA Concorde made just under 50,000 flights and flew more than 2.5m passengers supersonically.

A typical London to New York crossing would take a little less than three and a half hours as opposed to about eight hours for a subsonic flight.

The aircraft was retired in 2003, three years after the crash of an Air France flight in which all passengers and crew were killed.

70s Transport - Harder

```
P C M X I C H W Y I C E C N A R F R I A
T Q V J O P R E V I R D S U B C A N S E
X S N I A R T E V O R D N S F L V D J V
R X X W U G U A R D K C I W S I H C K B
T E H A N N A H Q B X L X Y S E N A L P
R O K Q Y T U Q V X W R E N I V L L I J
O G R Q E J L M S G D E I L P P A P A G
P A L B S L W I G A I B U D E L L I K O
S T Z L V O A U U B S D L E B F H G D V
N S H L M I L M L B H O D E F T I C A E
A C O E B G L R E U Y R D S T O P E D R
R B N U W I Z O K F O T C A N J G O D L
T H G M M M T L V D T Z N W B O C Z S A
P C P Z M H J L N A M S S E M R D F A N
C W K U I V H O S C W J R F W S A N K D
K R J R M Z C J V C Y E R I G T J B O E
O O T N K O X W X W O K D N F Z Z Q V L
L Y V W V J S K Q N R K A B H J J T W A
W O Y C N E W Y O R K B G H I Q K P R O
K Z J O O Z Y O B U N D E R G R O U N D
```

JILL VINER	FIRST FEMALE	BUS DRIVER	LONDON
TRANSPORT	CHISWICK	DEPOTS	THIRTY
WOMEN	APPLIED	HANNAH	DADDS
DROVE TRAINS	UNDERGROUND	GUARD	AIRLINER
CONCORDE	TWENTY BUILT	AIR FRANCE	BANGS
OVER LAND	TRANSATLANTIC	NEW YORK	KILLED

1947: Britain was struck this year by 'the perfect storm'. Record snowfall followed by a sudden thaw which culminated in heavy rain produced what is widely considered to be Britain's worst flood. Over 100,000 homes were directly affected and over 750,000 hectares of farmland submerged. The damages at the time totalled around £12 million, £300 million in today's terms.

1952: In August, the tiny village of Lynmouth, north Devon, suffered the worst river flood in English history. On the 15th, just over 9in (230mm) of rain fell over north Devon and west Somerset. The East and West Lyn rivers flooded and tons of water, soil, boulders and vegetation descended over Exmoor to meet at sea level in Lynmouth. The village was destroyed. The West Lyn rose 60 ft (18.25 m) above the normal level at its highest point and 34 people lost their lives.

1953: The great North Sea flood of January caused catastrophic damage and loss of life in Scotland, England, Belgium and The Netherlands and was Britain's worst peacetime disaster on record claiming the lives of 307 people. There were no severe flood warnings in place and the combination of gale-force winds, low pressure and high tides brought havoc to over 1,000 miles of coastline and 32,000 people were displaced because of flooding.

1963: Britain had the coldest winter in living memory, lasting for three long months from Dec 1962. The 6th March 1963 was the first morning of the year without frost anywhere in Britain.
It was so cold that rivers, lakes and even the sea froze over. On 25 February a record low of -22c in Braemar was recorded and 95,000 miles of road were snowbound.

1987: The Hurricane that wasn't supposed to be! Weatherman Michael Fish, like other forecasters, didn't see it coming. Eighteen people died and over 15 million trees were lost when in October, the hurricane-force winds blasted through south-east England. Meteorological research revealed a completely new weather phenomenon called the 'sting jet', a 100mph wind, the first to be documented in Britain.

WEATHER - EASIER

```
M F I Y A L L A F W O N S F E
M D N A L T O C S J X R Y Q H
W H B P K A L Y N M O U T H R
S E E N C O V Z G N F M W S W
E N N O U P T T F A O L E R F
D A I R W G G F W E R G A G E
I C L T S D N A L R E H T E N
T I T H X K I A P E C F H M G
H R S S S H D X X B A M E U L
G R A E R Q O V U O S J R I A
I U O A M G O V R T T H X G N
H H C Z X P L L Y C E L Z L D
H Z M H J I F X O O R Q C E B
Q P E R F E C T S T O R M B Z
J U V U N I A T I R B Y X D U
```

PERFECT STORM	**SNOWFALL**	**BRITAIN**	**LYNMOUTH**
NORTH SEA	**SCOTLAND**	**ENGLAND**	**BELGIUM**
NETHERLANDS	**HIGH TIDES**	**FLOODING**	**COASTLINE**
HURRICANE	**FORECASTER**	**OCTOBER**	**WEATHER**

OUR EXTREME WEATHER 2

2003: In August a new UK record was set for the 'Hottest Day in History' when temperatures reached 38.5c (101.3f) in Faversham, Kent. By the end of the summer, the heat had claimed the lives of over 2,000 people in Britain, mostly through heat stroke or dehydration.

An almost empty reservoir

1976: Britain had its hottest three months in living memory and it should have been the perfect summer, but with the continued sunshine came the worst drought in 150 years. Rivers dried up, soil began to crack and water supplies were on the verge of running out in Britain's most dramatic heatwave of the 20th Century. The drought was so rare, Britain appointed its first ever minister for drought, Denis Howell. He was nicknamed the minister for rain as the day after they installed him the heavens opened for the next two months!

2000: Following a wet spring and early summer, the autumn was the wettest on record for over 270 years. Repeated heavy rainfall in October and November caused significant and extensive flooding, inundated 10,000 homes and businesses. Train services cancelled, major motorways closed, and power supplies disrupted.

2007: Summer 2007 was the wettest on record with 414.1mm of rain falling across England and Wales in May, June and July - more than at any time since records began in 1766.
Although the rain was exceptionally heavy, climatologists say it was not the result of global warming. A report by the Centre for Ecology and Hydrology concluded the rain was a freak event, not part of any historical trend.

2004: A flash flood submerged the Cornish village of Boscastle during the busy holiday period when over 60 mm of rain (typically a month's rainfall) fell in two hours. The ground was already saturated due to two weeks of above average rainfall and the Jordan and Valency rivers burst their banks causing about two billion litres of water to rush down the valley straight into Boscastle. This led to the flash flood which caused total devastation to the area, but miraculously, no loss of life.

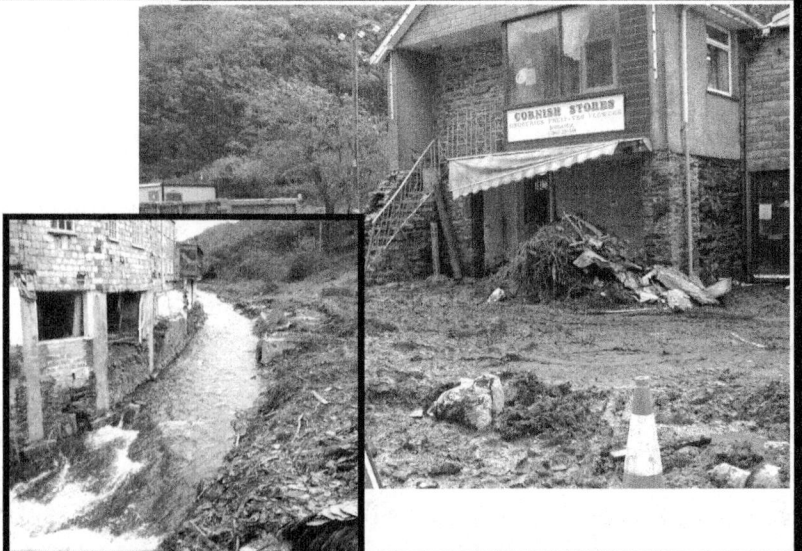

WEATHER - HARDER

```
Q Q R M P Q A L E C O L O G Y W A L E S
Y E W T Q U R E N I H S N U S Z L S Q M
A O I G L O B A L L D F X T H E B H F O
I B R E T S I N I M S Q L D W V T I A T
M E C A N C E L L E D T C O S A D D Z O
M G N I D O O L F A G P H Z E W E M B R
I N U N D A T E D F C H V B I T H K C W
Q P L W J J Q P V M R Q S X L A Y D P A
X N D W T S E T T E W V F R P E D I Y Y
T O Y V X N G A I S D A I T P H R S O S
H O T T E S T D A Y V O T D U V A R O J
Q D T A B L G P X E V T R P S F T U P G
Y C F P S V P O R R K O W N R J I P D R
R E C O R D S S E U U W P P E I O T B R
F L Y F N D H S T G M B H P W Y N E T R
U B A B O A E K H G J R N F O M D D F E
S V D W M R J T W K I B V U P R R X T M
H P C A P E V I S N E T X E Z E U Q R M
I G C P G N I M R A W R F T V S Z A Z U
Y E I E L S T S I G O L O T A M I L C S
```

HOTTEST DAY	**FAVERSHAM**	**SUMMER**	**DEHYDRATION**
HEATWAVE	**DROUGHT**	**SUNSHINE**	**RESERVOIR**
MINISTER	**HOWELL**	**EXTENSIVE**	**FLOODING**
INUNDATED	**CANCELLED**	**MOTORWAYS**	**DISRUPTED**
POWER SUPPLIES	**WETTEST**	**WALES**	**RECORDS**
CLIMATOLOGISTS	**GLOBAL**	**WARMING**	**ECOLOGY**

SOLUTIONS

PAGE 5

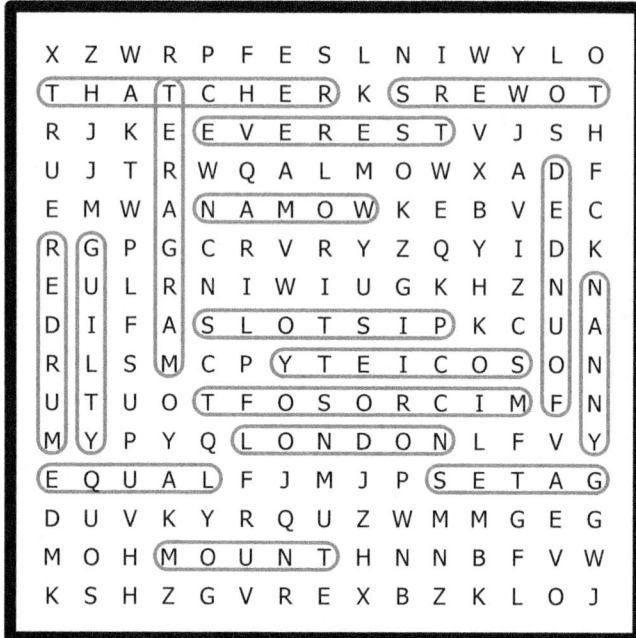

PAGE 7

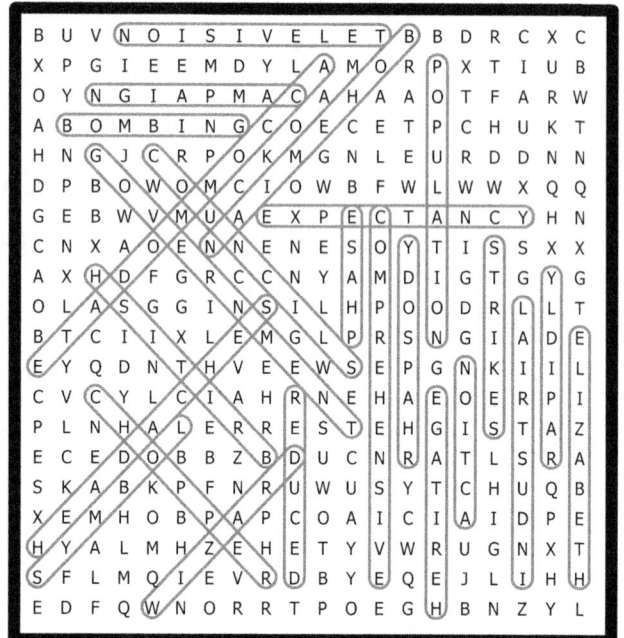

PAGE 9

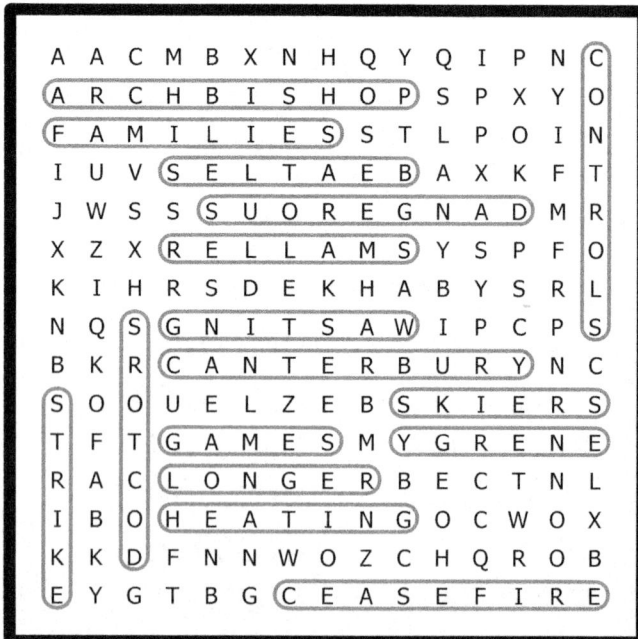

PAGE 11

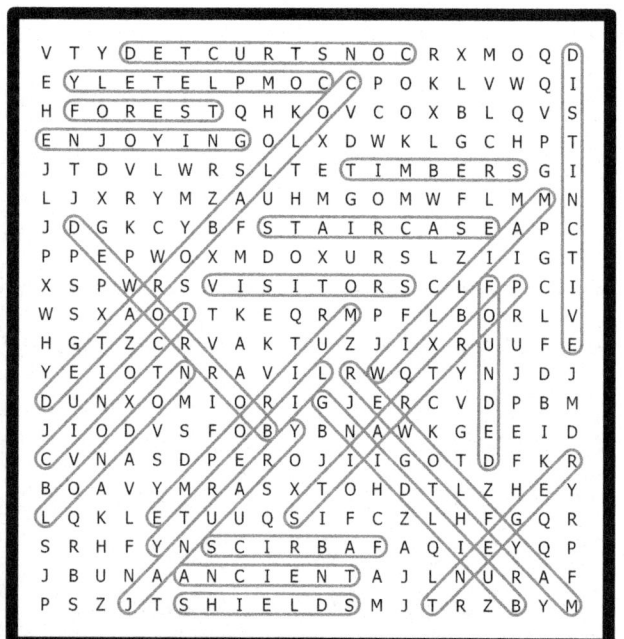

SOLUTIONS

PAGE 13

```
C T D G (C H U R C H E S) L S X
I K B (D E C A D E S) W M A X H
M O (I N D E F I N I T E) K R D I
O O S Y J R D (B L O C K A D E)
T I U Y (G A B L I A M) K X R B
A D V T J (G O L D E N) T Z V E
M G N I R A E P P A S I D C P
G J U L Y K D P G A Q D D Q R
N R D I E S (H G R U B N I D E)
Q A X B S A C A (B U M P E R) X
Y E F A X I J S (E A G L E S) U
Y L T I G X (L E V Y) B U R F P
G C W L R W E B W Z D P N U F
L U O U (N O I T S U A H X E) J
A N M (H I S T O R I C) Y P T V
```

PAGE 15

```
D (Y A W O L L O H) D I A D X M Y X T M T
P N S (D E N K Y L B E V T V R F O U Z V
S F C A K S K L F T I R V D O O C K R A
P R I R D G T R T S S W E U A I I E X F
R G T I D C Y M C H G I N B J D V S Z T
K U I N F N J O I N B D L Q M O C A O M
M D L G T H U R I N I O L A L E O P I W
R A O W T N E R S N S G Y U N W M S M E
L P Q E A E D B O Y T I E I O I I O R Q
L P O E A E D B O Y T I E I O I I O R Q
I P Q E A E D B O Y T I E I O I I T Z B
S S P P K C A E J N R O E R O N T P A B
N N A K P N W R P S L E D P A W E P E Q
U V Y O U O Y X O Q I E Q O E R S W M I
O R D O F (E C N A T S N O C R U F W D
C F C B B U C D O U W K L E C S O F W B
(D I S C O V E R E D) B L H U K F S W U B
Q D (T H A T C H E R) (E D W A R D) N F I S
M (R O S S E C C U S) (P L Y M O U T H) C C
```

PAGE 17

```
(A (E A (F L O O D) N U H C V G Y
(I D X M (N O D N O L) G R O P) M
R U T G U H B E I Z S E O R) Y
L C M V A J Y K T Q K K E O R B
I A B I E (F R E N C H) G G C I
N T V Q D G S D E C J F D E B Z
E I Z B U E N T V J D T I S R Z
B O G Z R S X Q E K R E R) B R
Z N M N T H X F R G U C B O J
(R E T S I N I M) P Q O Y G R P
P (S E I C N A D N U D E R S) T
U S Z Z H (F R E E M A N) Q X Y
K L G P (R E F U S E) (S E T A D)
X H (D E T A I C O S S A) C C J
(T E A C H E R) T V A K W F W H
```

PAGE 19

```
H K E Y R (S E C N A T S M U C R I C) Y A
S T X T G J W (R E T S A S I D) C X F E M
I V W (N A T I O N A L I T I E S) U O C N
L Y V N O (S N O I T P I R C S B U S) N U
O G Z N B F J A C F E G S Z W W P Q I L A
O O W F E H A F Z U Z L Q Q S L O T V N N
F B W L H N U M J A Z V T U W X L H N I C
T J V E L N I T I L V R O S J J I G O C E
E M F L T D G N L A I A L A C C C X F P
V I O E S F A K N S I I C T U C E X F P
R K R D Q E I O O E T A C T E N W A U R
G L B E L P S B C E I R N I P T E U M
O O A F A S U T H E S R T B A M A A N N
U D O D Q A W Q L M N I M F T N I Z E Y
M T I N M T J P C Q B G L V G I S F U R
T X T F Z I J K Q U M E A L H Y O K G K
D A T T O O A S U G Y R L A T N N E Q
R U N R F N F G T Q T P Q B K W K T Z E F
U M M J P S G J B B W D (S E U C S E R Q
```

SOLUTIONS

PAGE 21

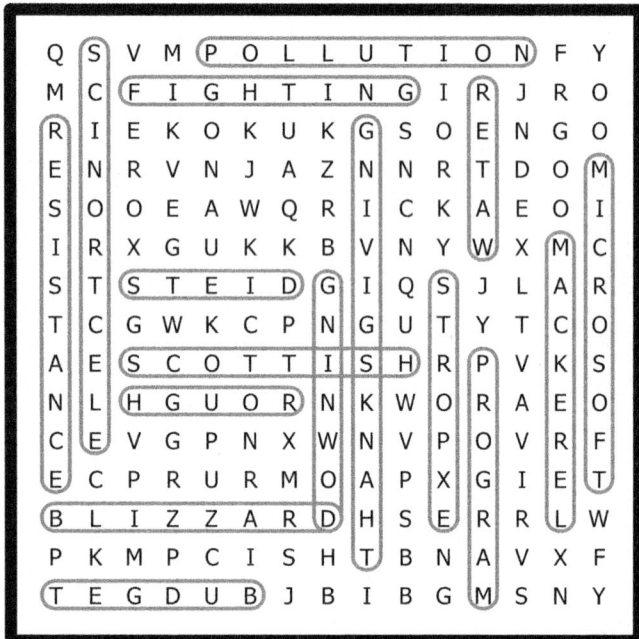

PAGE 23

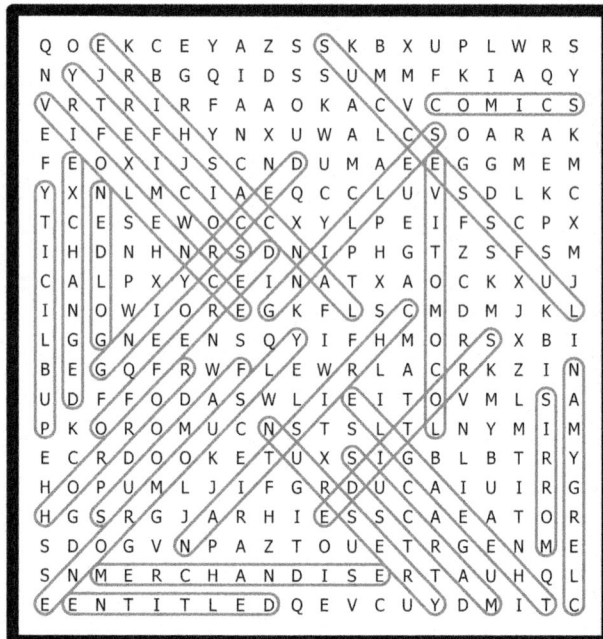

PAGE 25

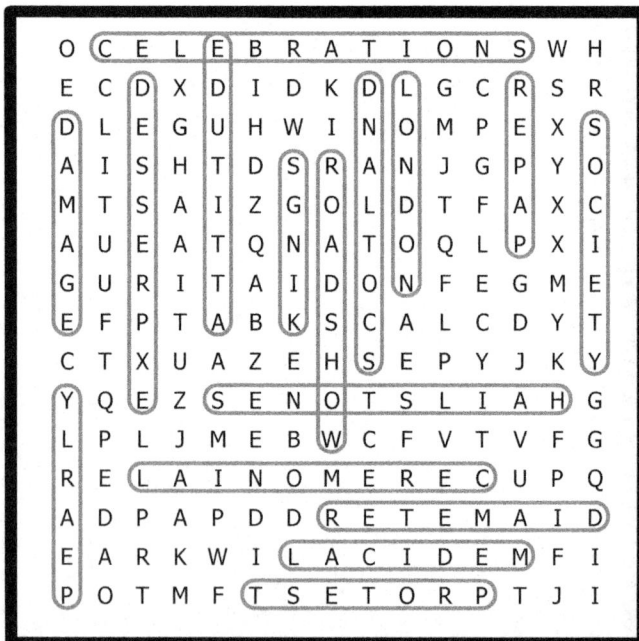

PAGE 27

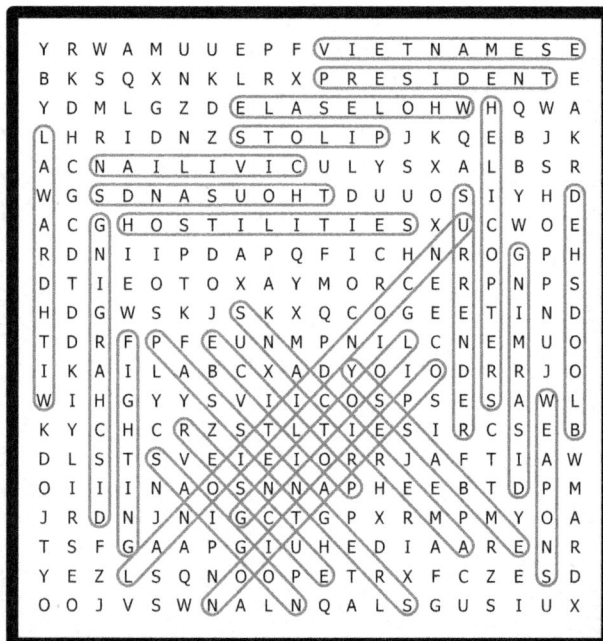

SOLUTIONS

Page 29

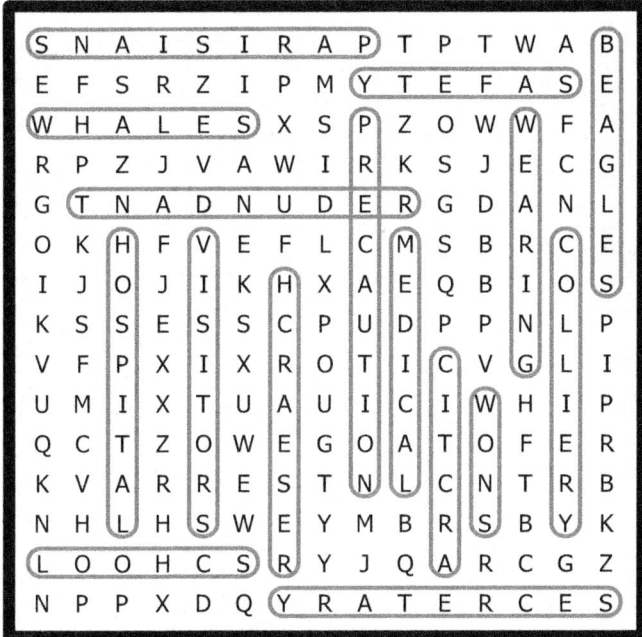

PAGE 31

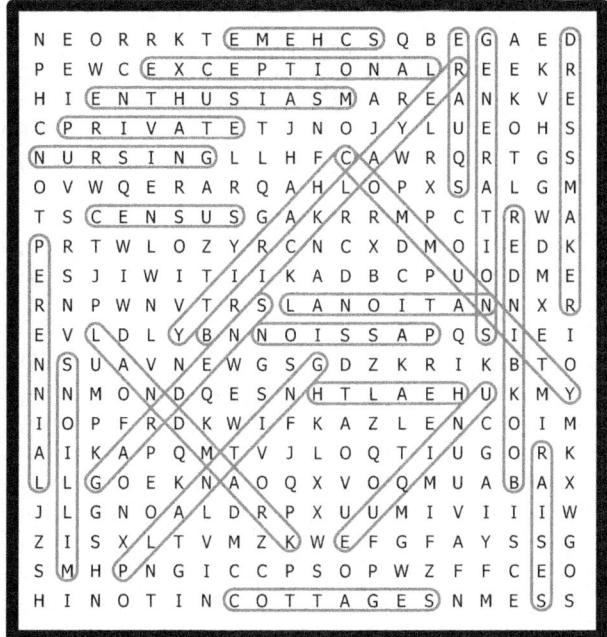

PAGE 33

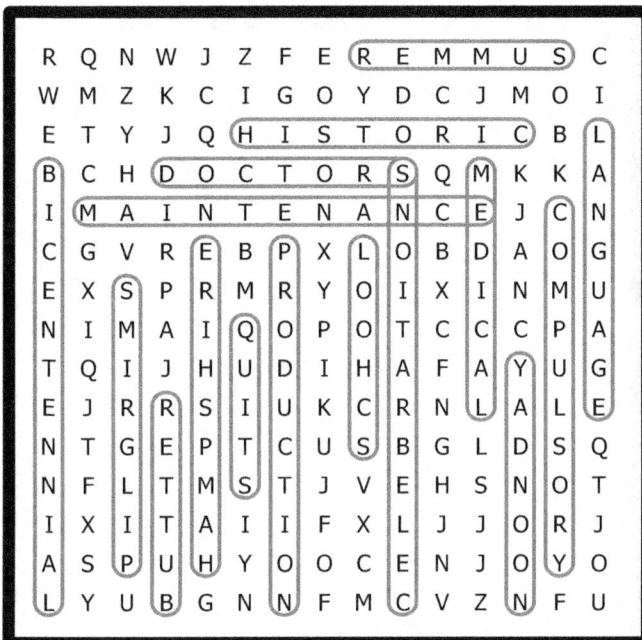

PAGE 35

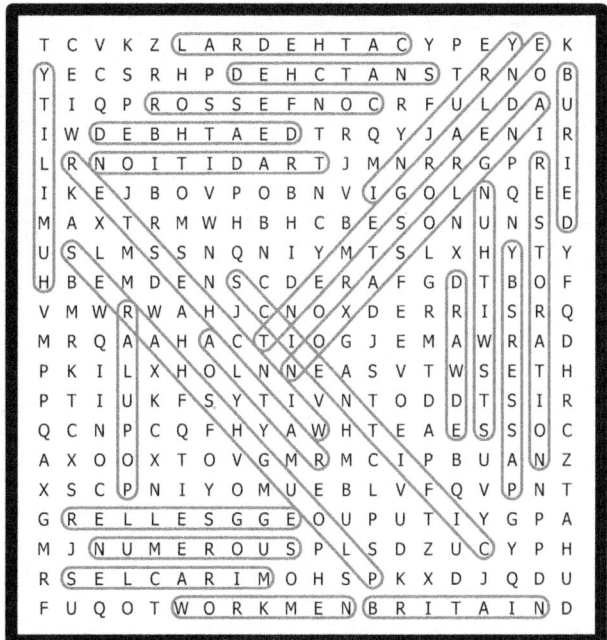

PAGE 37

```
O T R U A N C Y D H A V Z A S
K H L F C N U P S T A G E D S
C J Q R E L U C T A N T X W M
C V I O L E N C E G V W Q X A
B J K E W E A T H E R Y Q B L
G N I T N E R A P Q I T P C L
A S L E E P C J M I P P X I P
G L O W M R P Q L R V S Q R O
D N F R E G N I S S I K N O X
E I R E L B A E G N A H C X Y
S E A P E G D E L P E H V S V
U G L Y H T L A E H D G Y I Z
M A W W E A F E K P R L F H O
A S L O B M Y S A J O V L E E
T N O T S N I W B Z K X D X C
```

PAGE 39

```
E S R O T I S I V E S Z L G W B S G X W
V K V S B E Y W U Q T V K X A P E Q J K
I N B T H I O N D L F P F A S V R C Q C K B
T O H G G I M S I N O P N I H M P Y D F
A I S I C U L O L N T O G U V C L N E B R
N C Q T X V M A C O T U T N A C T Q C I
R U T O K E K H A M N P L A O T Y R B G
E L D P O K L T R O P E L V L N Q I O A E
T A O M F Y E D E E A M Y F H I R U O V P
U A R U B Q T O G W N N F R I N G E D N B
A P B O P R W T V I I E R T A E H T Y Q
L I T E R A T U R E A L A R U G U A N I
D N I B O R Z I Q S T H N W E E S K D I
U S E C N A M R O F R E P P U Z J H O Z
F H G R U B N I D E E X Z P U L T T U S
L A V I T S E F Z T F V Q W C D M U N
E E T T I M M O C G N B Q R J K Z A S Z
L H O W U Q G V L H E U H I S E U N E V
```

PAGE 41

```
Y V X I U U T M D E B M O B H
D U N X Z K G L Z B J K S R T
K Z O M H S E L D E E N R E E
H S I Z O C S T F A H Z I T I
K J T U O H D Z S W T I V I V
P X A E S P E N E H I F O O
R J D F E G A R A D T E R S
O K N I W I M S R B V R G E
T O U O D V A T M I W B N T
E A Q M I N E R P E R S L P W
S M I L O S Q B R H N J E S F V
T J L T E M L E H H K I L T
L W L A R R E S T E D S X D L Z
D K G N I T N I A P Q S F N L T
M
```

PAGE 43

```
Z W E W X B V L A F L J T E X O N O T N
F E G W A A U L H A E M D Q N P I A O R
P X V P C C E S V F U G Y N I R A L P T
I F R U I A I I N O S A E S C E L G B S
T N G F H T T W C J A E I D K L I T O E
R T E C I S O L S T I C E R N A I G O P
A R I R E B U W Y S U B E W A G O N T
D M B F H H X H I P A M B B M I D U E M
I O R E T R A U Q M M I A E O U L T B
T K E V B J C Y C U S A L X Q U J S E
I K D J X G V T S S P D Z E L S P B A R
O W K O V T N D S F G A N N A E D O F
N H D G I O I I J E A R X A Q H E U A O
A Q G P R M X M N S V M O U S R C U S G
L C E L E B R A T E D R I M O U L I K T
L H C V Y P P M O S T N A L N M O Y M L
Y N Y C A E I W T O R X K H I W B H Z D
H G O O S E T C I X V L O K X E P R T W
V O N A I W D E P Z O M P H G O S T A G
K N T A U T U M N F J D U P S Z S E Y U
```

SOLUTIONS

PAGE 45

```
F M A R C H E S S G U X E E J
R Y N R E L S Y R H C I P L L
O O G C X X E D R O C N O C X
T G N H A S T R I C T X O J A K
P U I A J K T J T F J O T Y B
L R L M C N H D O A A F D K D
U T L B E T N O T F R C K N Y A
C X I I U D M P T C O G R L M
S F B O F R H U H R N Z B M A
N K A N M A Q X I E K I N A H
O J L S M G H K L V E P X E U
S G T H E F F P M O R E S S M
I P I I J O J O C H S E N W A
B Z B P O O E D E E R W S A P
S L U S Q R G S Z W K S G J M
```

PAGE 47

```
Q J I B R I T A I N H N S C P D Y Z U X
A O C H O C O L A T E G S L N J F E U Y
A E B I E W D X U B E C N E U Q E S T H
N W B J K K O O A T D O M I N A N T O R
O S K G T L M U P E Y Z W Q N C E R A Q
E V Z Y N S A U Y P E W N G E X A G D N
L G Y J T A H M O R L V I W P T L J E O
L K N R V U E I M A O S P S I A O L A Q
A B O I G H M P C Y N T F O F W S I Y X
G M M W T C S I O E R Z C A W O J L X G
Q W E H T A R N R R H O R I N E A Q K Y
N Y R I V O R N O J U T T S V N W T H U
C T E E T R A O C N Q E W C O S K D K I
F D C S K V U C M C N Z R I I A M D C K
N O I T A R B E L E C A T P C V N H F A
O H R L L H B X Q D M I C I W A I O I G
L A R I M D A U D X D M L N S Y H H O R
V K W V B T T B N A E P O S E Q E Y J K
C X E C N A R F R C E F E C O U Q E A E
P O J Y N Y E T S R C I N O E L O P A N
```

PAGE 49

```
M J P S L I M I T S Z A J N O
Q W O M H H A R D S H I P S Y Y
K O L N G N I N I A L P M O C
N N I V D N D E R I S E D B D
O I S X N E Q O N G N E E U Q
I D H B E L J M B E S Q H O R
S N J B M H Z D O M A E R T S
O O I X O W V A I O F Q R T
L L F M W Z T J Y Z V D P W L
P E C A N R U F K D R I V E R
X N I G U S H E C I L O P M C
E A S S E L K C E R R P E O O
Q T I C S E V I W E S U O H E
U O B T E G D U B S R C K S C
J M K B K A Y E Z Q X H L W H
```

PAGE 51

```
S O H O N O U R G F S T E A M I N G S P
J E S U S N X U S G N I D D U P D L N L
A Z M E G N I N U O L H E R U T S I O M
D W N I I S I N T E N S I F Y P T R B H
L X N O I T I D A R T T F D U P N S R A
L M L S H I Z D P R Z R E R O A E P A N
Y Z U N T Q F X N X Y L I R B I V X M D
H A O U Z N B B U K L T R X R A D Q T Y
D P A C L P E K S E S I Y U R I A U Y
G R I G T O N T A D G U N Q G S O I R
M I C N O B U R R E E E O E G E L I S
X K P R B T S H L C R C V C M H Q R X C
P I S R R J A E X E M Q G U B I K U T E
N N A Z U R L D W Y S N P L L V O E N
B G N C Y D E T C E P X E I A D C P J G
X N X M G N I P P A R W E V N R E F N Y
Y D A H S Z F S V I M O X W C E O O K G
T E Q Y R Q U F L D K O V W A G Q M
H H C P T H J H X U E Q R M O P L A Y J
```

SOLUTIONS

PAGE 53

```
S T N E M N R E V O G W W P H
U L I S M E L L Y N B V F H N
J A U S T R A L I A N Z O F O
B X H U A I J O Z M S D Z O R
S T H G I L F E B E C G T R L
J I K X Y S L X N R H S U B I
O L Q F X G Y X E I O A K I Z
A D I S A S T E R C O L D D I
E S E E H C W J P A L V V D S
Y G E Z U X C F M N S A F I L
L P R C J F E M A L E T X N A
K W C H R I S T M A S I K G N
C B B G D H I C B L O O D Q D
I D D B S B O N Q Y D N Z I W
R H A B T W E S I D A R A P T
```

PAGE 55

```
U J X L I G H T S I K C E L T I V F T R
F L N M C N P U A D S O I D A R Y A D G
L O T O G H A X Q A P I U Y W X A K B P
Q D E K I P C K G V D A S E C O N D D H
P O N R D V C L K E Q Z X M G H F E O U
Q N M P N G U A Q E W J H R E A F S C G
T G C F U L P M Q U V R A W D I L W O C
K X U R R O E T A G I S R N K L I K M R
E U N B R X D P N T A O T O Y N U N A I
E A T I U P O O U E A Z S P A R T A N S
R G U K E J G C A E W K A T V T R Y I B
G R A Q N K S X A X L T C I F E A P P U
E E L R J Y T V F C P K E V I C O J U P
E V U M B T R A G L A F A R T G V E X E A Q K S
N L M B T G E N T L E M A N G D E B K S
S C J N T O R P Y F W R I J B W B D O O
```

PAGE 57

```
T Y B G S Z F H H J P F M P N
E T A G R E T A W D I K K V M
L Z U C W C O M M U N I T Y R
C I Y L I A D H D U O E J P R
B C R H O D E S I A N C T I E
F I N S D L A N O D C M D G T
H L N I S B M O B U A B L Y S
C B E G A G N I V A E L M W E
T U L R E S T A U R A N T F H
E P E C O N O M I C I K C D N
K E N G A P T J X K J A M J A
S R Y N B F O G H T A E H O A
E K L Y V X V R Z T A J I G M
N O S L I W M N A E P O R U E
Y A D L A M I C E D B A Z S Z
```

PAGE 59

```
P N D S U D Q B C N C E Z P C A K Q F L
E T E P Z J U F K R C W U U B M E I U T
S V Y H P I U O I W M K N D J F G C R Z
S T R E E T S B W R S E V E R E P T T C
T H A T C H E R I V E Y V I K K E E Y V
V S J P Y Z Z L N S A R K T M G W Z L
I R S Z N E C R B N E A B D R P W F H L
E I S K B L C T A J C E T R E R M Z O R
T O G S U P D N D C W K E R O S B A L E
N V J T A O U U V R Z J A G R K M X E V
A R Y A X E A O Z Y O T C E X T E R L I
M E F T D P I C B K U U F A E K P O Q I
T S H E L N N B R R J F G N R P S J U S
N E J C U O N I E T K E Y U L Z H M T C R X T
E R U O N I E S C W C B T W E W S X
D Y G A E R O R C M Q O G R K Z
L O W O T H I A Z O L I A F S P O R C K
O N Z H H M T H S D R I B Y D A L G V T
Q W P K E G Y U U P X B T S E R O F O D
```

SOLUTIONS

PAGE 61

```
R Y M A E R C E C I S K E M O
P C U U W X T R I M P H O N E
T M R L V T R U O L O C U M Y
N K Q G N I L B R A W O C F G
A S I U L Q E C A L P E R I F
L G K S S R E G A N E E T S P
P N V P P H C U O C Q V F H R
F I T I D M A G I M I X L F O
G S N D N M F B I T F F O I S
J A O E X O R K S U I B R A P
F E R N J E O N U J G A N E E
M R D V J T E X T Y G L L R R
O C I H I X Z H W B R X L R I
H N V X F G E F M V J Y G S T
O I W N M K R W V K M G O N Y
```

PAGE 63

```
K D B A N D S A N D A C T O R S Z X B I
F S A E T E N E O Z R S E C N E I D U A
Q F K N X I D E M Q N O I S I V E L E T
V K G D S Y Q M W U E Q B N B B B D E D G
A C C E J E F U G T M T B E Q V X F M R
I E Y C N C T X Y E O B F R R V S U O M
V D A A I J S T J N E N E P I T A Q T K
I O D L L A G X E T H L J D M Z K C F G
L E X P B E S I I E T G E O R C F M M D
O R W E O E G R X R Y O L H H O Q L R V
G E H R G M U R Q T G A U V E N O O O P
A T O L R O Y I O A I M F H O V F M D O
T S M V V M B Q M I G Y S G C D I W S S
A Y Y E A W T J E D N E U S K E W X T T
R Q F F G S J A M O V E R T N T I E E R
I C A P T I V A T E D H C L J R O M D S
P Z B Z O Q I U H N X T C U G D L R A S
O S T C F A U T G T L H U L F G D R X
N L A N W O T M O O B X S W Y A X V T A
G U W N O H J J T E E N A G E S J S U S
```

PAGE 65

```
I W U F E S T I V A L J E H W
A T P B J R A M N P L J I Q N
O L J S N D H I A B S B T K P
Z A D E L T I C M J R A S N A
I U R C I V E R K H E A I T T
T R E A B M F O L R D G R R O
T E I P R A G S A O A H I T C
O I N M R S R F K B N T T I A
R C I C Y M I T K Z I A R I R
A E L O U X Q F L X N G G N R
V I J E V I T A G K Q G R W D E
A P Y R U B N O T S A L G P W T
J F S B L U E P E T E R R X L
C K N W C C U B H J S U I P S
```

PAGE 67

```
C I Y C O C Y W H P Z K S R V R L N Q M
D A L Z G V P Y M R A F B Z M I T U T E
B D F I R S T E M P E R O R F V K V K T
X Q P D A H W E G I G K V E S Q M T R R
S S B M L P U T R V F Q S O J Z N Y M O
R E R O B D P E L U C I N A S Y M T V P
E H O S R A P T D C A E H K O C K N E E S
H C I Q A E E Z O L L E S Y I C A M Q T L
C R R B T T S R L E S Z E S R I S P O T I
R A F S R T Y M C U U Z D R L W U I A T A
A P A J O A A N K A A O F H N O A S W R N
U W R T E C E S D S H P Y A N R S B A U T
X I Y X E O V A E T A U E S A T E Y H T U
W J Q N C T O A G L R L F U I S C H C Q I
R R G Q A T C A W I E O M O C U C A P I
N C H I F A R L L V P J P H U A U N E P
Z C E W C D U F I E O M M T L V S D A
S U T H E R L A N D C S E S R O H E Y E
T U D N M P A V A R O T T I H A S W A P
```

SOLUTIONS

PAGE 69

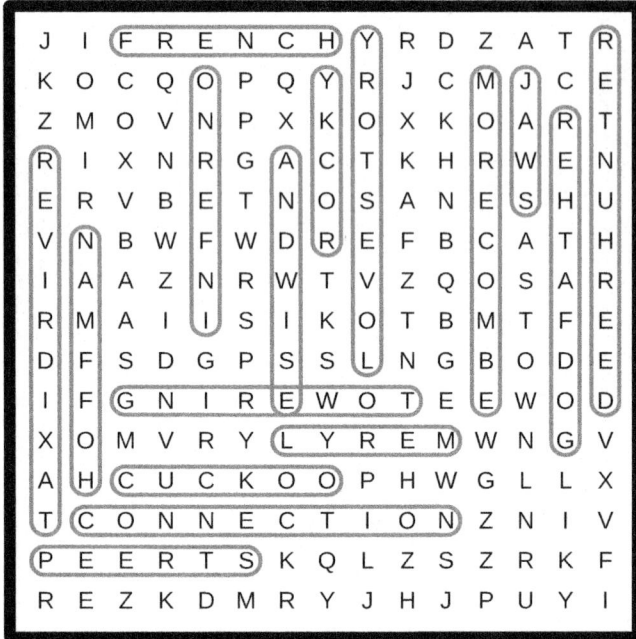

PAGE 71

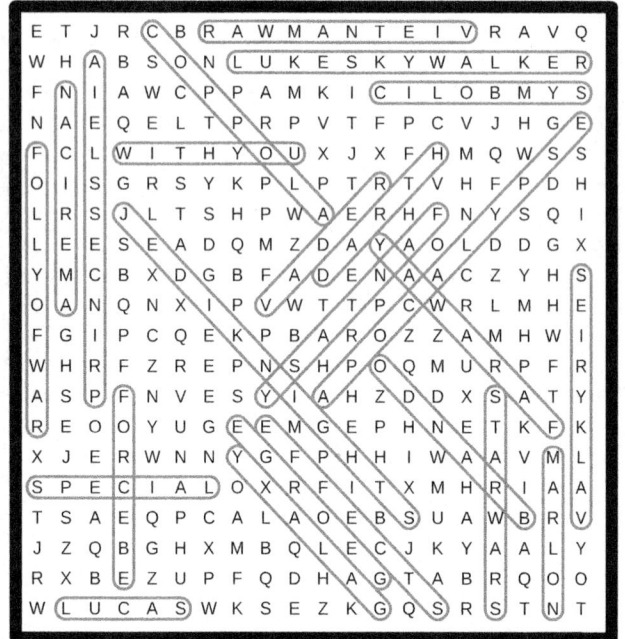

PAGE 73

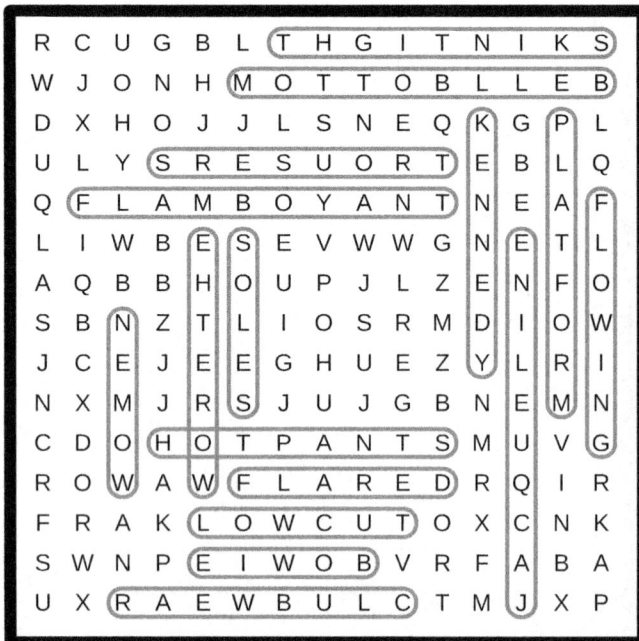

PAGE 75

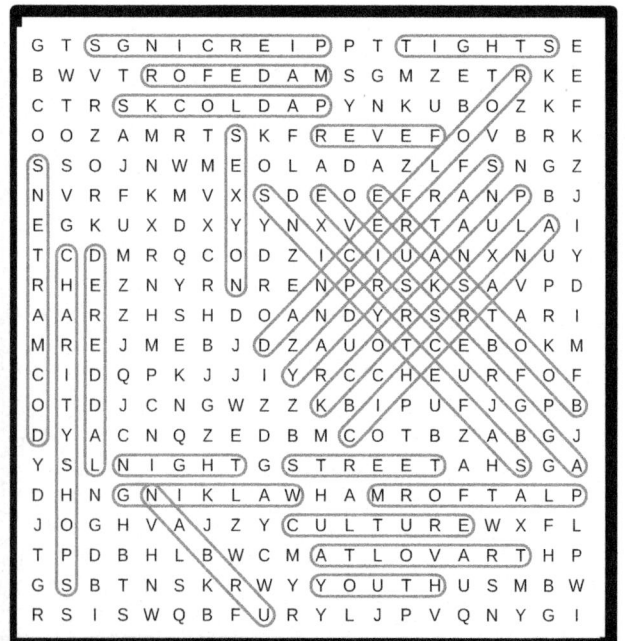

PAGE 77

```
I I C W I W N N U S A W S I T
I C I U R E T L A H V A G Z N
O N E W S R O U N D Z I V S F
Q S K T E L O I V A R T L U T
M N I L I P S M O R N I N G D
T O O G N I T A R Y G P P F I
L I Y A D R U T A S Y Q E T S
W T E D M O N D S P L V K Z C
G I J F K S U O R O M A L G O
H T E L X M Z F M H W D I Y T
N E T A K N I E N O H P I B H
L P Z P Q O C A R T O O N S E
Z M E S P A N D E X X Q O T Q
B O T R A V O L T A R G Q Z U
S C G N I T T U R T S C K Q E
```

PAGE 79

```
X M U P W P B R B O T T L E C E P M M X
N X L R U R C W K F A T A L H F F Z A S
L K R Q Y C L X S J F V Q H W M U N E V
V T R M B C P I F T F O F R I S B E E H
Q A I F E P N G N A E N S V W C G H V O
B R O K E N R E L O Z L Y R X V N U W L
Q Z E Y P A Y L G N I P K S E Q I J E S
N D M S P M O K Y R B T M O O G N E T E
F H S H V U A B W K E L A K O Y N A B G
Y B I D T A P D B I I M S M O B A A Y D
M C S O Z V I E Z F A F E G R H L F D I
M E L E D S H R L Z I L I Q O P H L O N
C W D F U N H U Y C X O S T A X F Q A G
A F L S R H R S N B O O L C G A J N B A
D V E A M Z J I T H J R N V F E P X I G
G D E C V H V E Y T I C I R T C E L E L
A L R P E V U L D X Z C L F F S X Q M A
W A R N I N G S X R A W R A E L C U N S
M L F G N I L I P K C O T S E U N X M S
M I W S O T H W Y L L A I T N E T O P E
```

PAGE 81

```
W T F Y E L L O W V T C X E U
D M W E N E H T Z F L D N K K
O R A K O Y S O F C V K H T N
V U T P O E E X C C U O Q K K
T G E R B L E U T K U S J B O
R C R J H S K R S H M T N W Y
O L E N E E R V E U E R T G I
U W O G O R R V R E S L A R F
B N O D B P S I B E S L G N L
L J T I B S I S N E U K E F K
E Z M R I I Z I E T Q Y T U N
D C G B R V M A O P A D V P N
D R W S P L B N R K Q H L K J
O X S E Q E Z O A B W D O E J
B V R E V O B E C V Y Y V N L W
```

PAGE 83

```
B T T K N O W I N G M E K O J V C Q P I
T D L W I E O Z F I R R Q A N T N N H S
Z K E Y D O S P A H R L M T F E W X E R
S U Z C R E V E F T H G I N W G A B N R
O Q H Y A D R U T A S B M T E S T D O F
U N K Y A E K A T S Y R O I I U E C M C
N Q Z W T V Q C A N Z N Y Q G C R L E M
D A R H P O Q E P S J A B Q J C L S A M
T T D B S W D C M O H F N D U E O J A M
R L U R L P Q H A S Q Q A G S O C L M A
A O B M Z O I N A A G X F Y I S G Y R A
C V T O L C D Y J N E D I K M L F L M
K A A N L N B K N X R C H K P E W E A R I
F R B A I A E N B N Z U E T H L D H J A
Q T I W V D C E A U Z N R O F Z A O O K
Z N H I I T W N U Y S J E M N O N F G B
W H E T A T F D A J Q G T J M H J C A K B
J O O A C O D C C B E Q E U A V I F G G
T N H K M C V N O M F O R X N N E D N
A A E T F C Q T G A D I Q Z D U G Y L Y
```

SOLUTIONS

PAGE 85

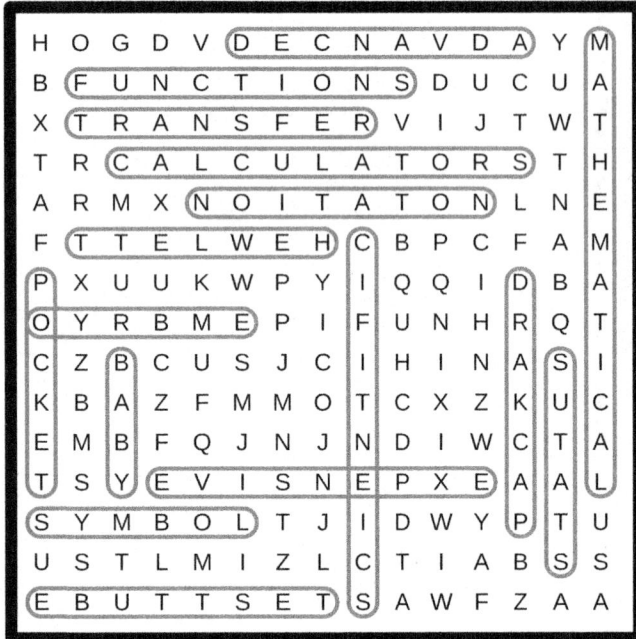

PAGE 87

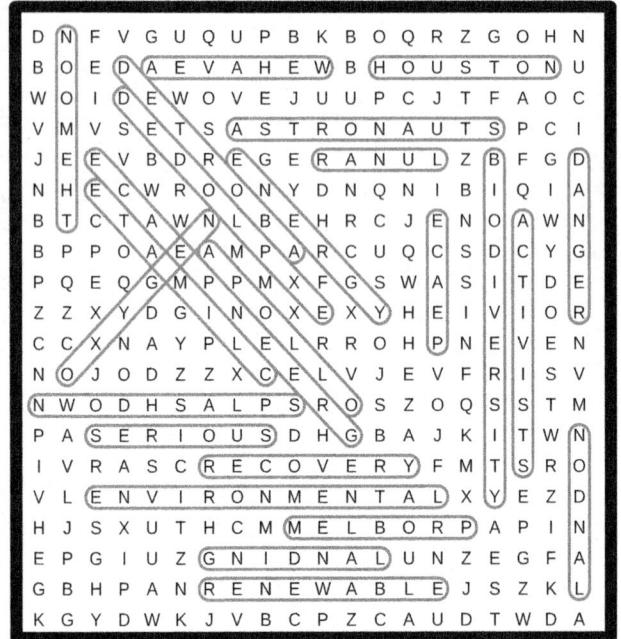

PAGE 89

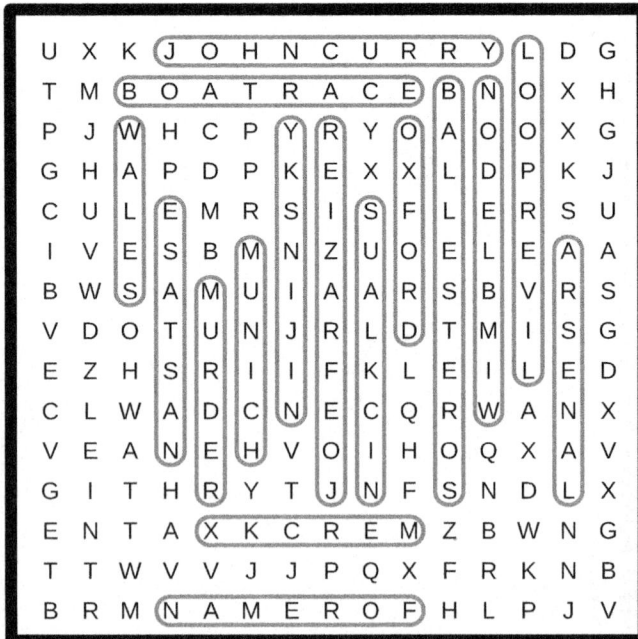

PAGE 91

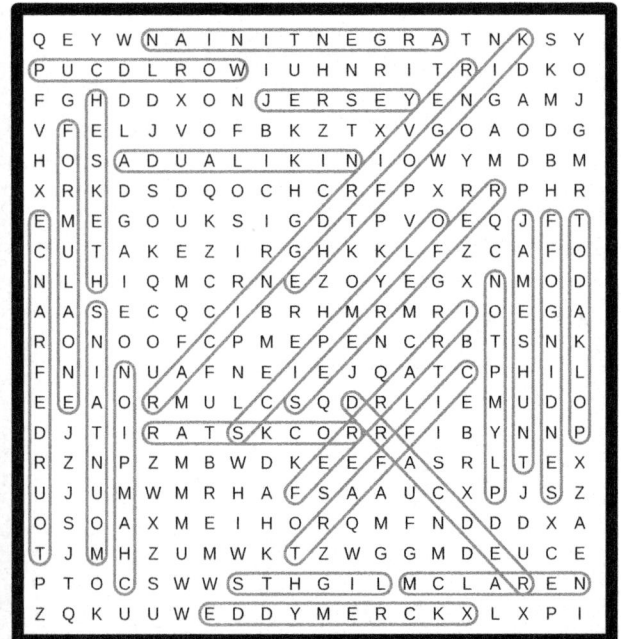

SOLUTIONS

PAGE 93

```
M F P T V A I C O N I C K U Z
T A E S G N O L G F G G M J P
T W O L E K P S S P U V R I D
J N U S T A D I C N Q A K M I
W G N I L L E S T S E B S Z X
Y N N U S M A C H I N E S F N
G A H F T E J O B M U J F X D
E L A O Y D N G I E R O F U D
A L B M Q A V S N B P T I U Q
R E K V T C O R T I N A T D C
L G Y R I E B I M P O R T X Y
E R D I E D U P H G I E L A R
V O U M M F O T B B Y P M U D
E F T D S O Y L M A H B D F V
R C M V R E P P O H C G E Z F
```

PAGE 95

```
J U H N J K N G Q G O B A R E G V S B T
T F S H J C N R H R Y Y U T R U I P I R
D H X K I I E A I R Y D H K L A C N K O
S V Q K E W M X D F C I E D Z R O Q M P
P O C U O S O B L R L C R Z D N M K R S
I F H R S I W K O T C S N O X H C T Y N
K C D A U H W N Y Y D O A V C T O Y W A
G B O I S C D U K D U R R E I R R W E R
M J B Q W O W L A B X A F T T A D Q N T
G E Z M N P A D B W P O R R D N E A J S
A I R L I N E R M B I U I A E S N L I S
K A R M D A V O U H S J A I P A V V L G
O M B U S D R I V E R M U N O T S K L N
F I R S T F E M A L E O J S T L K R V I
L K W J O V E R L A N D V F S I V I B A
M W O O K V X M H A N N A H Y N L W N J
F Y P V D W Y S A K A X Z G I T L Z E K
Q W Y Z D N U O R G R E D N U I E F R C
C P Q E H U A P P L I E D B J C D A O K
I W J M S B T W E N T Y B U I L T N Q M
```

PAGE 97

```
M F I Y A L L A F W O N S F E
M D N A L T O C S J X R Y Q H
W H B P K A L Y N M O U T H R
S E E N C O V Z G N F M W S W
E N N O U P T T F A O L E R F
D A I R W G G G F W E R G A G E
I C L T H S D N A L R E H T E N
T I R S H X K I A P E C F H M G
H R S E R Q O V U O S J R U L A
G A E R Q O V U O S J R I G N
I U O A M G O V R T T H X G L D
H H C Z X P L L Y C E L Z L B
H Z M H J I F X O O R Q C E Z
Q P E R F E C T S T O R M B Z
J U V U N I A T I R B Y X D U
```

PAGE 99

```
Q Q R M P Q A L E C O L O G Y W A L E S
Y E W T Q U R E N I H S N U S Z L S Q M
A O I G L O B A L L D F X T H E B H F O
I B R E T S I N I M S Q L D W V T I A T
M E C A N C E L L E D T C O S A D D Z O
M G N I D O O L F A G P H Z E W E M B R
I N U N D A T E D F C H V B I T H K C W
Q P L W J J Q P V M R Q S X L A Y D P A
X N D W T S E T T E W V F R P E D I Y Y
T O Y V X N G A I S D A I T P H R S O S
H O T T E S T D A Y V O T D U V A R O J
Q D T A B L G P X E V T R P S F T U P G
Y C F P S V P O R R K O W N R J I P D R
R E C O R D S S E U U W P P E I O T R R
F L Y F N D H S T G M B P W Y N E T D F
U B A B O C G J T R N F O M D O F E R E
S V D D W M R J T W K B H U P R R X T M
H P C A P E V I S N E T X E Z E U Q U J
I G C P G N I M R A W R F T V S Z A Z U
Y E I E L S T S I G O L O T A M I L C S
```

1975 Calendar

January
Su	Mo	Tu	We	Th	Fr	Sa
			1	2	3	4
5	6	7	8	9	10	11
12	13	14	15	16	17	18
19	20	21	22	23	24	25
26	27	28	29	30	31	

February
Su	Mo	Tu	We	Th	Fr	Sa
						1
2	3	4	5	6	7	8
9	10	11	12	13	14	15
16	17	18	19	20	21	22
23	24	25	26	27	28	

March
Su	Mo	Tu	We	Th	Fr	Sa
						1
2	3	4	5	6	7	8
9	10	11	12	13	14	15
16	17	18	19	20	21	22
23	24	25	26	27	28	29
30	31					

April
Su	Mo	Tu	We	Th	Fr	Sa
		1	2	3	4	5
6	7	8	9	10	11	12
13	14	15	16	17	18	19
20	21	22	23	24	25	26
27	28	29	30			

May
Su	Mo	Tu	We	Th	Fr	Sa
				1	2	3
4	5	6	7	8	9	10
11	12	13	14	15	16	17
18	19	20	21	22	23	24
25	26	27	28	29	30	31

June
Su	Mo	Tu	We	Th	Fr	Sa
1	2	3	4	5	6	7
8	9	10	11	12	13	14
15	16	17	18	19	20	21
22	23	24	25	26	27	28
29	30					

July
Su	Mo	Tu	We	Th	Fr	Sa
		1	2	3	4	5
6	7	8	9	10	11	12
13	14	15	16	17	18	19
20	21	22	23	24	25	26
27	28	29	30	31		

August
Su	Mo	Tu	We	Th	Fr	Sa
					1	2
3	4	5	6	7	8	9
10	11	12	13	14	15	16
17	18	19	20	21	22	23
24	25	26	27	28	29	30
31						

September
Su	Mo	Tu	We	Th	Fr	Sa
	1	2	3	4	5	6
7	8	9	10	11	12	13
14	15	16	17	18	19	20
21	22	23	24	25	26	27
28	29	30				

October
Su	Mo	Tu	We	Th	Fr	Sa
			1	2	3	4
5	6	7	8	9	10	11
12	13	14	15	16	17	18
19	20	21	22	23	24	25
26	27	28	29	30	31	

November
Su	Mo	Tu	We	Th	Fr	Sa
						1
2	3	4	5	6	7	8
9	10	11	12	13	14	15
16	17	18	19	20	21	22
23	24	25	26	27	28	29
30						

December
Su	Mo	Tu	We	Th	Fr	Sa
	1	2	3	4	5	6
7	8	9	10	11	12	13
14	15	16	17	18	19	20
21	22	23	24	25	26	27
28	29	30	31			

We have books for people born in almost all years between 1940 and 1980.

To see the full range scan the QR code and be taken to the Amazon page showing them all.

We also have framed prints to celebrate the year of your birth.
These make stylish and interesting gifts for birthdays, wedding anniversaries and other special times.
Each can be personalised with the recipient's name(s).

Scan the QR code to go directly to the framed prints.

Printed in Dunstable, United Kingdom

63836315R00065